A Fancie

REX RABBIT

by
JOHN HODGKISS

Many years ago I was told by an irate
exhibitor that what I didn't know about
rabbits would fill a book.

Here it is.

Copyright 2003 by
Coney Publications
Chattisham, Ipswich, Suffolk IP8 3QE

Other titles in this series:
The Beginner's Guide to the Cashmere Lop
  by Jean Wolstenholme.
The Beginner's Guide to the English Angora
  by Barbara Pratley and Yvonne Hobbs
A Fancier's Guide to the Netherland Dwarf
  by Phil Birch.
Rabbit Nutrition
  by Virginia Richardson.

In production:
Lop Rabbits by Geoff Russell

ISBN 1-898015-05-8

Set in 11 Baskerville,
printed and bound in Great Britain
by K.D.S.,
Ipswich, Suffolk.

Contents

Foreword

Coney Press invited John Hodgkiss to write this book some eight years ago but to their great regret publication was subsequently delayed for commercial reasons. But here it is at last, a wonderful celebration of the rex rabbit for the fanciers of the new millennium.

They are indebted to the late John Sandford – author of the *The Domestic Rabbit* – for proof reading the first draft and offering suggestions. Sandford thought this was the best book on the rex rabbit ever to be written, a sentiment echoed by one of the fancy's greatest rex judges Mrs Joyce Potter, who kindly agreed to write the Foreword. Sadly, Mrs Potter died in May 2003.

It was in the early 1940's that I first saw, and fell in love with Rex rabbits.

Those rex belonged to Tommy Leaver, one of the greatest breeders of both rex and normal fur and an outstanding figure and leader of the Rabbit Fancy. Encouraged by him, and by Harold Dowle, another such man, I bred many varieties  of both rex and normals, having at one time 500 hutches. Visiting innumerable Shows, I had the privilege of book stewarding for both Tommy and Harold, learning a great deal in the process.

After a period of such tuition I embarked on a judging career and was very fortunate to have been asked to judge at every type and size of show, including all the classics in every part of the country.

I have read the manuscript with great interest and in parts some nostalgia. 'A Fancier's Guide to The Rex Rabbit' is certainly the most detailed and interesting book to have been written about Rex.

A full study of its pages cannot fail to help all breeders, indeed all aspiring judges. I wish the book (and the author) every possible success. I am sure it will be invaluable to all fanciers interested in rex.

Preface

HAVE YOU EVER STOOD within earshot of the public at an Agricultural Show or similar, and listened to the comments when they come to the Rex pens? "What beautiful colours!" "What beautiful coats, just like velvet!" All this, without even touching the rabbits: if they are given that privilege, their admiration is doubled. We thus have, in our chosen breed, something which is unique, which makes an immediate and obvious impact: if this book can do anything to increase the number of active breeders, it will have achieved its purpose.

What I have set out to do is to write something which will appeal to as wide a cross-section of fanciers as possible. The complete novice who has never kept rabbits at all; the fancier who at present keeps other breeds and is thinking of starting in Rex; the existing Rex fancier who may be contemplating taking up another colour; even the established fancier who could be expected to know more about the Rex than I do: I hope they will all find something of interest in these pages.

What I have NOT tried to do is to write a complete manual on rabbit keeping. This has been done several times in the past, never more thoroughly than in *The Domestic Rabbit* by John Sandford; no fancier should be without a copy of this book. What I have tried to do is to include enough basic hints on management to enable anyone to make a small start in Rex; knowledge can then expand as the stock is built up. Whilst we are never too old to learn, and we learn best from our mistakes, I have attempted to point out some obvious pitfalls.

Neither have I tried to give a complete history of the Rex. Other than in artwork credits, very few names are mentioned, except where they are particularly relevant to any particular variety; only once have I referred to a fancier still living. There are very many people who have made major contributions to the progress of the Rex, but to mention some and not all would be most unfair. The object has been to give a broad enough background to be able to judge past achievements against today's Rex; it will be seen that the popularity of the breed has risen and fallen in a series of peaks and troughs, sometimes for no apparent reason.

It is a matter of great regret that some of our oldest varieties have become so rare as to be in danger of extinction. So much so that a great deal of space has been allotted to measures whereby they might be recovered, even to the extent of including a chapter on simple genetics: to bring some of the varieties back is going to require at least an outcross, if not a complete re-creation.

This would be a most worthwhile assignment for anyone who is perhaps more interested in breeding than showing; many judges would come into this category, with their limited opportunities to exhibit their own stock. With very few exceptions, the inheritance of colour in the Rex follows a well-charted course; however many varieties we may have lost, they could all (apart from the Astrex) be regained by anyone with a little knowledge – and a lot of patience and hutch-room!

There has never been a consensus of opinion on whether we should refer to the various Rexes as different breeds, varieties or colours. Some would hold that all Rex are one breed with separate colour categories; others insist that, as we do not, for example, normally breed Ermines and Havanas together, they should be classed as different breeds, and still more would class them as varieties within the breed. Certainly we must regard all the rough coated, Satin or Mini-Rex as separate varieties, but with that proviso I have used the three terms almost indiscriminately – if only to avoid repetition.

Self Rex

Black. *Exhibitor: Mrs Jean Ross*

Blue. *Exhibitor unknown*

Ermine. *Exhibitor: Rutland Stud*

Havana. *Exhibitor: Andrew Wray*

Top of the Show Awards

The Black Rex has been the most consistent winner of Best Rex and Best in Show awards over the past decade, followed by another Self Rex, the Ermine

Lilac Rex. *Exhibitor: Mrs J Thornton*

Also in this category: Nutria Rex, (believed to be extinct, no photos available)

Shaded Rex

Sable Siamese. Exhibitor: *Claret & Gold*   Seal Siamese. *Exhibitor: Bernard Welford*

Smoke PearlSiamese. *Exhibitor unknown*   Tortoiseshell. *Exhibitor: Ms Gwen Soutar*

Tan Pattern Rex

Fawn Rex. *Exhibitor: Rosebay Stud*   Orange Rex. *Exhibitor: Mrs E Cakebread*

Tan Pattern Rex

Sable Marten. *Exhibitor: Bernard Welford*   Seal Marten. *Exhibitor: Tony Peacock*

Fox (Black). *Exhibitor: L & A Appleby*   Smoke Pearl Marten. *Exhibitor: Mervyn Bevan*

Left: Otter (Black). Exhibitor: Mrs A Scott Coomber. Right: Otter (Lilac). *Exhibitor: To be Traced.* Other recognised colours are Blue and Chocolate

NB: Fox Rex – other recognised colours are Blue, Chocolate, Lilac.

Agouti Rex

Castor. *Exhibitor: Rutland Stud*

Chinchilla. *Exhibitor unknown.*

Cinnamon. *Exhibitor: Caneddy Stud*

Lynx. *Exhibitor: D & S Bulman*

Opal. *Exhibitor Harry Hopkinson (Pipnip)*

Agouti Accolades

Most consistent winners in the Agouti section have been the Chinrex and Castorex.

In 1972 a Chinrex was best in show at the London Ch Show's prestigious event at Alexandra Palace, winning a Hoover washing machine.

In 2003 the Castor above was Best Rex at Bradford Ch Show following a run of best in show wins

Other Rex Varieties

Dalmatian Bi Colour. *Exhibitor: Ian Gerrard*   DalmatianTri Colour. *Exhibitor: D Bumford*

Himalayan. *Exhibitor: D & N Sword*   Harlequin. *Exhibitor: N T Dewar*

Above left: Satin *smooth coated Cinnamon*. Right: Satin *smooth coated Ermine*.
Both exhibited by Shlegal and Davies

NB: Other colours recognised in Himalayan are Blue and Chocolate. Satins can be shown in any colour or pattern recognised by the BRC standards. Regret no photograph available of the Silver Seal, believed to be extinct.

Rough Coated Rex

Astrex (White) can be bred in any recognised colour. *Breeder unkn own.* Above right: One of the first Opossums to be shown. *Bred by Mr Cover.* Below: Opossum re-launched at Bradford Ch Show in 2000. *Exhibitor J Wood.*

Mini Rex

Ermine Mini. *Exhibitor: Mr Johnsons*   Black Mini. *Exhibitor: Odin Stud*

The Mini Rex is shown in all colours recognised by the BRC. Above: latest introduction is the Broken, seen here being assessed by the BRC Breeds Standards Committee

THE ORIGINS OF THE REX

UNLIKE MANY BREEDS, the Rex can chart its history back to one pair of animals. These are generally recorded as having arisen in a litter of cross-bred Belgian Hares belonging to a French Abbé, M Gillet, in 1919. Despite inherited weaknesses, and difficulty in getting the stock to breed, Gillet persevered and got them standardised as Castor Rex – Castor from the Latin for Beaver, or brown, and Rex, Latin for King. Hence, "King of the Browns". That is the generally accepted story: in truth, not even the date will stand up to close scrutiny!

I am indebted to the late John Sandford for supplying copies of some very early correspondence and articles from France on the early history of the Castor Rex; we both felt it important that this information, coming as it does almost "straight from the horse's mouth", should be preserved.

Firstly, Gillet never claimed to have bred the original animals. As Abbé of Coulange, in the Sarthe region, he appears to have devoted at least as much time to outside activities as he did to his religious duties (shades of Gregor Mendel!). He was a very well known breeder, exhibitor and dealer in animals, mainly rabbits, and as such was in a very good position to get to know of any stock with commercial possibilities.

Much evidence exists that short-coated specimens occasionally turned up in litters of the rabbits most common in that area, namely the Geant Normand or Picard. Whilst this breed may have shared a common ancestry with the Belgian Hare, they had had their own standard since 1895, and obviously existed well before that date. Weighing 9 - 11 lbs., sometimes much more, they were obviously well suited to peasant commercialism for food and fur.

With the primitive travelling conditions which prevailed, it is not surprising that the majority of stock became very inbred, a factor which Gillet later claimed to be the major reason for the appearance of the Rex.

So, although Gillet's first Rexes were certainly obtained in 1919, there were almost certainly others which had appeared earlier; due to their rather unattractive appearance they duly made their contribution to French cuisine!

The actual rabbits which are the true ancestors of what we have today were born in the rabbitry of M. Desire Caillon, who was what we would call a small-holder in the village of Luche-Pringe, near Coulange. More importantly for posterity, his son worked on Abbé Gillet's farm, and told his employer about the strange specimens his father had bred. Just two of them, not litter-mates, although it can be inferred that they were born in successive litters from one pair. As far as can be ascertained, they were the only two Rexes which Caillon bred, and once they weighed two and a half kilos Gillet bought them to see if he could get them to breed true.

What attracted Gillet was the shortness and silky texture of the rabbits' fur, the colour was quite a secondary consideration. When he eventually named the new breed as Castor Rex, he implied "King of the Beavers" to refer to the texture which he considered superior to that of the Beaver which at that time was the most commercially valuable fur.

It is commonly believed that Gillet's first two animals bred true from the start – as we would expect today. Again, this is not true, as normal coated specimens were produced in the first and second generations. Gillet always regretted in later years that he never bred from these normals, so we can only conjecture as to the reason for their appearance, which I will do in the chapter on genetics.

Gillet's main preoccupation was to improve the appearance of the animals, which he described as rather bizarre. Very long in the ears, narrow in the head, overlong back legs and twisted front legs; together with lack of fur in the nape, only a supreme optimist would have considered this sound foundation stock!

Gillet, however, always maintained that his rabbits were by no means unhealthy. Accusations that they were prone to rabbit syphilis were countered by statistics that they were neither more nor less so than any other stock in the region. Litter sizes of eight or nine were common; one of his customers had in fact had a litter of sixteen, all reared by the mother and one foster. They were no more difficult to breed or raise than any other variety; how much of this is established fact and how much salesmanship on Gillet's part is open to question!

Two litters were obtained from the original buck and doe,

following which the latter died – why, we don't know. By mating father/daughter and brother/sister Gillet succeeded after two years in eliminating the normal coats, and then set to work to remove the physical abnormalities. This he did by crossing with Tans, Beverens and the Giant Normandy, and refused to show any of the new breed until he had at least got rid of the twisted limbs.

Thus, although he sent a pelt to the Paris Show in 1923, which created great interest, it was not until the following year that he felt confident enough to exhibit a live specimen. Not one, but five, which appear to have taken the first five prizes in the class for new breeds.

In 1926 he appears to have sent at least 30 exhibits and made a clean sweep of all the prizes except Best in Show; he was not allowed to compete for this as there had not been a separate class for Castor Rex. Since there was no official standard until at least two years later, that was hardly surprising!

What is surprising is that when a Castor Rex Club de France was formed in 1928, Gillet's name does not appear; Caillon was an honorary member, but that appears to be the only connection with the originators. Since Gillet's interests were very much commercial, he may well have made political enemies: Article 5 in the Club's constitution - "All religious and political discussions at Club meetings are forbidden" - may be significant! For whatever reason, l'Abbé appears to have been effectively side-lined, even the standard he put forward being rejected in favour of one submitted by Prof. Kohler, who became the first President of the Club.

Kohler was a Professor of Languages at Strasbourg, and had a very large establishment of animals; until the arrival of the Rex, goats appear to have been his main interest. He obviously continued Gillet's work on outcrosses, and showed the first coloured Rex at Strasbourg in 1926. He soon became an even bigger breeder than Gillet and the two must have been considerable rivals in the field. What subsequently happened can only have given further proof to the saying that a prophet has no honour in his own country!

By the time the Club was formed, a variety of colours had been produced: Ermine, two types of Black (one an Otter, the other from the Alaska), Blue, Havana and Himalayan. The latter deserves a closer look, but it is interesting to note in passing that, of the two types of Black, the Otter, despite its grey belly, was reckoned to have a better top colour than the Selfs derived from the Alaska.

The Himalayan has a somewhat chequered history; known in France as the Russian, it originally came to this country as a rather woolly coated meat rabbit under the name of Siberian. The Rex variety apparently first appeared in Normandy in 1925, bred by a Miss Delagoutte. No scientific examination appears to have been carried out on this stock, but it is highly likely that this is an identical mutation to that which occurred in the same breed, in the same region, in 1927. This stock belonged to a Madame DuBary, and she did take the trouble to fix the strain. It was by working with this strain, together with that of Gillet, that Castle and others proved the existence of at least two distinct mutations (see chapter on genetics).

REX IN THE UNITED KINGDOM

Whatever Gillet's disappointments at home, he appears to have had no difficulty in establishing a lucrative export trade, and his first customer in Great Britain was the Lady Layland-Barratt of Torquay. Another member of the landed gentry who was one of the first in the field was Lady Watson of Wharfedale, who not only became famous for modelling a coat made from Castor Rex pelts, but went on to become very much a leading light in the first club to cater for the new variety.

The involvement of the so-called upper classes has by now disappeared. In 1926, when the first imports were made, it must have been essential, as the prices paid were in the region of £50 (at least £1,500 in today's devalued currency). Rumour had it that the first doe which Lady Layland-Barratt imported was barren; her Ladyship's comments, if this is true, have not been recorded. Undeterred, she made

Mrs Jack Arney's Ermine Rex buck White Knight, winner at Crystal Palace in 1931 (*The Rex Breeds of Rabbit: Watmoughs, 1931*)

Early example of a Chinchilla Rex   *The John Sandford Collection*

several more purchases in that year, but does not appear to have shown any of the stock.

The honour of being the first recorded exhibitors of the Rex belongs to Goodchild Brothers, later to become very well established in Crawley as probably the most successful commercial rabbit keepers ever known in Great Britain. From a pair purchased in 1927 from Lady Leyland-Barratt, they entered at least one Castor Rex at the Great National Show in Leicester, on 24/25 November the same year. The judge (Geo A Drake) described it as "the sensation of the show, a truly unique creation". That he was not too enamoured of the general appearance of the animal may be judged when he only placed it sixth!

Whatever Gillet may have claimed for his stock, the early imports were certainly not reckoned to be beautiful. The bare napes, chopped-off rumps and long ears were still characteristic, only the twisted front legs having been largely eliminated. The British Fur Rabbit Society, which was at that time the nearest thing the fancy had to a controlling body, were not sufficiently impressed at that time to recognise the breed, although strangely they did recognise the

Chinchilla Rex in 1929. Interestingly, this first standard called for a weight of 5½ to 6½ lbs., and a coat length up to one inch. Faced with this intransigence, the Rex breeders decided to go it alone, and on March 15 1928 called

Lady Layland Barratt's Black Rex buck "Knossus", bred in 1929, reached an adult weight of 4¾lbs. (From *The Rex Breeds of Rabbit* published by Watmoughs in 1931)

a meeting in Birmingham with the object of forming a club for Castor Rex. This was duly agreed, except that, to cater for the other colours which were being introduced, the name of the club became the British Rex Rabbit Society, which did not affiliate to the B.F.R.S. until 1931. Lady Watson was not only the first Secretary and Treasurer, but also interim President. This honour eventually went to the Countess of Harewood, thereby cementing the link between Rex and Royalty. (Whether Lady Layland-Barratt declined, or was not offered the post, was not minuted.)

Squirrel Rex, bred and owned by Miss C E Hendry of Fife and advertised at stud in 1931 "for a fee of 17/6 – special terms for several does from one stud"

By now, most of the Normal Fur breeds had been rexed and several colours – such as the Lynx and Opal – introduced which had never been seen before in any guise. Progress in gaining general acceptance was however, slow. Whilst there appears to have been a fairly steady demand from the fur trade, exhibitors had to fight very hard to get a decent classification for the new breed at other than the major Classic shows.

WORLD WAR TWO - THE BOOM YEARS

AFTER THE OUTBREAK OF HOSTILITIES , the picture changed completely. With meat rationed, there was every incentive to breed more rabbits than ever before, and thousands of newcomers were introduced to the hobby.

Many, of course, relied upon cross-bred stock, but enough people were convinced of the extra value of the pelts of the pure-bred Fur breeds to raise their horizons, and the Rex gained the greatest benefit from this influx.

Despite difficulties with travel, the number of shows also dramatically increased from the pre-war figure. The motto seemed to be: "Show the best and eat the rest".

In 1941 the Southern Rex Rabbit Association was formed, not as a branch of British Rex but as an independent body. Whether this was simply due to any natural antipathy between North and South is very difficult to say at this distance: there was certainly a feeling in the South (which persisted for many years after the War) that B.R.R.S. had not taken sufficient advantage of the upsurge in interest, and a separate club was needed.

Perhaps the subsequent figures speak for themselves: by the end of 1944 Southern Rex had 1,000 members, and 17 branches covering all the Southern Counties, all of which held at least two shows a year. In contrast, British Rex never had more than 400 members, mostly concentrated in the North. It is, of course, a matter of conjecture that, if the amount of effort that Bernard Rawlins and Lloyd Denman put into building up Southern Rex had gone into B.R.R.S., we might have had a united Rex fancy approaching 1500 members by the end of the War. We can only assume that they tried, and failed, to get support from the National Club before going it alone.

Although the virtues of the Rex as a furrier's rabbit were always extolled, at this distance in time it does not appear that a proper industry was established, either in this country or the U.S.A. Whilst there were any amount of processing firms which - at a price - would dress the breeder's own pelts, a large scale market for the raw skins never seems to have existed.

THE POST-WAR PERIOD

After the War was over, there was a period of euphoria which, as I recall, was very short-lived. A new Government came to power, promising a land of milk and honey; in reality, rationing continued at a still harsher level, even bread and potatoes being restricted, which had never happened whilst the fighting had been going on!

Needless to say, encouragement of 'back-yard' rabbit keeping was still the order of the day; everyone with four breeding does was entitled to a weekly ration of bran, a scheme administered by the B.R.C. on behalf of the Government. The subsidy received for this was a very useful source of income for many years.

Thus, the need for clubs at all levels still existed. Whilst the easing of travel restrictions meant that the big classic shows were re-instated, the exhibition side was very much a local affair. Relatively cheap rail costs meant that it was possible for many people to send stock far afield by rail, whilst still attending their local venues with their 'second strings'. By this means, fanciers were able to support Specialist and Local Clubs at one and the same time, and the specialist clubs continued to expand.

None more so than Southern Rex, its thousand members and seventeen Area Branches now augmented by a number of Colour Clubs or Circles. Inevitably, this led to a demand for it to be given national status, which duly happened in 1947, when it was renamed the International Standard Rex Rabbit Association. A rather strange choice of title, some might think, although, as it only meant a small change in the initials, not a lot of money had to be spent on re-engraving the trophies! More importantly, many of the rarer breeds or colours, such as the Opal and Cinnamon, which I.S.R.R.A. had always supported, which had been recognised in other countries, but which B.R.R.S. had always tended to ignore, now had an improved status: hence the 'International Standard' in the title.

Members of I.S.R.R.A. were responsible for getting together a quantity of stock to re-establish the fancy on the Continent, chiefly in Holland.

At the same time as all this was happening, most of the Colour Circles were given National Specialist status, whilst others – like the Chinrex and Ermine – were formed from scratch. It is also from about this time that one can chart a gradual falling off in membership throughout the fancy.

There seems to be no one reason why this should have happened. Some today blame British Rail for the withdrawal of privileged pricing for exhibition animals, but this policy did not come into effect until very much later; it only accelerated an existing trend. Likewise the withdrawal of bran ration – the numbers claiming it had already fallen to an uneconomically low level before it was abolished. Rather must there have been a combination of causes. Many must have kept rabbits almost solely for fur and flesh: with the gradual improvement in supplies of other meats from the butcher; and the failure of the fur industry ever to become properly established, the incentive to keep rabbits was removed from many.

Other hobbies – and the coming of the great god television – took many more away; to many people the rearing of rabbits and poultry represented a connection with war-time austerity which they were only too glad to sever.

We were thus left with a nucleus of real enthusiasts, many of whom had had Rex since the very early days, plus such new recruits as they could muster. Not only did they have to compete with other hobbies, but there was now further competition from within the fancy itself, in the shape of such new varieties as the Satin and Netherland Dwarf, to be followed soon by the New Zealand White and the Californian for those of a commercial bent.

From being the novelty breed and Mecca for the experimenter, the Rex had now, so to speak, become part of the Establishment. There was, and still is, an element which felt that we already had enough varieties within the Rex and that no more should be allowed; with no scope for experiment, many people who might have come into Rex twenty years earlier now went into other breeds.

Was the existence of two National Specialist Clubs, catering for all varieties (the two 'Umbrella Clubs'), plus separate Clubs for many of the individual colours, in the best interest of the breed?

There was always a school of thought that questioned whether it was in the best interests of the breed to have two "Umbrella" Clubs. This is not to mention the Universal Rex Club, another potential rival to British Rex, which came into being soon after the War, but swiftly disappeared into oblivion. Therein, I believe, lies the core of the answer – market forces: if a demand exists, it must be fulfilled.

At the time when other breeds such as the Belgian Hares and Angoras were being forcefully urged to amalgamate their existing clubs, British Rex and ISRRA successfully fought to be allowed to continue their separate existences, and continued to do so into the twenty-first century.

I count myself among the many who felt that, given the role of the BRC as arbiter, the two clubs should be allowed to go their separate ways unless and until an overwhelming majority of the rex fancy decided that amalgamation was in the best interests of everyone.

The officials of both clubs came to the conclusion at the end of the 1990s that, given the steady decline both in membership of both bodies, and rex entries at all shows, their members should decide whether the two clubs should join forces. As a result, we now have the United Kingdom Rex Rabbit Club as the sole "Umbrella" organisation. It is up to us all to make sure that the amalgamation will work, as there can be no going back.

Whether or not the undoubted ups and downs of the Rex had a political element is, therefore, debatable. Were the Rex of yesteryear – if more plentiful – any better than those being shown now?

I very much doubt whether the average quality of the real boom years was very high at all – commentators on the post-war era seem unanimous in agreeing that, as the numbers came down, so the quality went up.

A major decline in the fancy in general, and rex in particular, set in during the last two decades of the twentieth century. Many of the big Agricultural and Municipal shows disappeared, whilst many indoor venues became unavailable. The combination of the animal rights, health and safety, and anti-smoking Mafias must take much of the blame for this.

I feel that the best balance of quantity and quality probably existed in the 1970's. Today, we have far fewer rabbits being shown, and a smaller gene pool to breed from. Whilst it is probably true that colour in most varieties is as good as it has ever been, those big, bold rabbits (the only ones which can carry the proper Rex coat) are few and far betweeb. How to breed more of them is the substance of this book; logic decrees that we ought first to decide how they are best housed and managed.

HOUSING

THE REX, being a fairly large rabbit, needs fairly large quarters, although there is no need to go to extremes. It is obviously unkind to house any animal in such a way that it has barely enough room to turn round; it is equally unwise – and wasteful of space – to give it so big a hutch as to make it feel insecure.

Whilst it is true that a wild rabbit is continually on the move when above ground, it does not necessarily follow that the tame one needs or wants to exercise to the same degree. The wild one, when in the open, has but one object – to satisfy its appetite and get back home before it is taken by a predator – and must therefore cover a lot of ground quickly. Underground, it probably does not utilise much more space than it can lie down in. The tame one needs just enough to be able to move around in comfort, any excess will hardly be used, and will result in a greater loss of body heat to its surroundings.

In practical terms, hutches should allow 1000cm^2 clear floor space for every 0.5kg of weight of an adult rex, thus giving a stock hutch of approximately 100 x 60 cm (*source, John Sandford's The Domestic Rabbit*). Breeding hutches can be four or even five feet long, but there is no point in making them deeper or taller than the stock hutches.

Countless designs for hutches have been published, ranging from the Heath Robinson to the highly exotic: don't worry, the rabbits haven't read the books and, provided that certain basic parameters are met, will be quite happy with what you give them. Space has already been covered; they also need to be dry, fairly warm and free from draughts. Several materials will meet some or all of these requirements: I have seen hutches made from bricks, breeze-blocks, packing cases - even hardboard, but there is no doubt that wood is the most satisfactory all round material.

Never be tempted to try to keep Rex on wire floors; the feet will go bare quickly enough as it is. A good solid base is required, treated with preservative; a creosote substitute is the most cost-effective, but always give it at least two weeks before putting stock in it – the fumes are lethal. For indoor

Outdoor hutches built by the late Dennis Arrand

use, quite a light grade of plywood can be used – some I bought in 1978 can only have been made from three-ply materials, but have stood up to some very severe service. A completely removable wire front is the most convenient, but for outdoor use a covered sleeping compartment will be needed.

It is an open question as to whether hutches should be housed in the open or in a shed. There are many who believe that all Fur rabbits grow denser coats if housed outdoors, provided that they can keep dry and out of draughts. Certainly, low temperatures, in themselves, are well tolerated by the rabbits, but damp cold can be fatal. It is probably more to the point that the owner will tolerate wintry weather much less well than the rabbits will, and they are liable to receive less attention just when they need it most. Whilst it is usually possible to find a sheltered spot for one or two hutches to begin with, most fanciers will eventually want a shed – or commandeer the garage.

Any hutches for external use will obviously need to be of much stronger construction than those used indoors. Half-inch tongued and grooved boarding is the minimum thickness to be adequate, which will need to be well treated with a wood preservative, then covered with roofing felt. Some form of shelter, to keep off snow and driving rain, is essential.

Block of eight indoor hutches under construction. Note the removable partition which converts a double to a generous single for breeding purposes.

VENTILATION

Outdoors, there is obviously no problem in obtaining adequate ventilation, but great care must be exercised with an indoor rabbitry to ensure a free flow of air. Nothing will cause a rabbit to lose condition more quickly than a dank atmosphere laden with ammonia fumes – it does nothing to improve the owner's health either. There must be a good vent at the apex of the roof, with the upper half of one wall left open. Fine-mesh screens, to keep out pests, are sometimes recommended; in my experience, a mesh small enough to keep out insects will soon become so clogged with debris as to keep out all the air as well!

LIGHTING

There is much evidence to suggest that adequate light is essential if rabbits are to be expected to breed successfully; most commercial breeders will use artificial light to simulate at least eleven hours of daylight throughout the year. Few fanciers would go to that extreme, but most would agree that electric light in the rabbitry is virtually essential for the owner, if not the rabbits. Just try looking after a block of outdoor hutches on a cold, wet, February night armed only with a torch and you will soon agree too.

SUNLIGHT

It might be thought that allowing our rabbits to sunbathe is a kindness: it is nothing of the sort! The wild rabbit will take great pains to avoid direct sunlight, and we should take the same care in siting our hutches so that the sun can never be directly on them. At worst, heat-stroke will ensue; even if this is avoided, the pigments in the fur will be attacked and the colour will fade, thus ruining the rabbit for show.

BEDDING

Wire floors being taboo with the Rex, some form of bedding must obviously be provided; in fact the choice of bedding is probably of greater importance in the Rex breeds than any others.

The problem, of course, is the prevention of bare patches on the feet; in many cases these are hereditary, but even the best-bred stock can soon be ruined by unsuitable bedding. The modern tendency is to use soft-wood shavings, several inches deep, and to replace the soiled portions as necessary, sometimes on a daily basis. This is all very well if the rabbit only uses one corner of the hutch as its toilet; it becomes a bit of a nuisance when – with most bucks – soiled bedding is thrown around all over the place. Other possible disadvantages stem from the fact that the shavings can be so easily scattered, and the rabbits seem to love to dig down into them. There may well be sharp edges to the shavings, which will damage the fur on the feet, and once the rabbit has dug down to the floor the whole object of the exercise is defeated. The material used must be best quality white wood – anything else is bound to stain, whilst shavings take so long to rot down that composting them is hardly practical and potentially good manure is lost.

The biggest disadvantage must be the cost. Whereas in the past most fanciers could obtain shavings free from their local builders yard, the majority now buy them by the bale. In my part of the world, a bale of shavings now costs five times as much as the equivalent weight of hay. Nevertheless, for exhibition Ermines they are probably essential, but for anything else alternatives ought to be considered, if only on the grounds of cost.

SAWDUST, if obtainable, is very absorbent, but is hardly suitable used on its own. If used, care must be taken that it does not contain any sharp slivers of plastic material.

NEWSPAPER is also highly absorbent, free from impurities, and will rot down much more quickly than shavings. With so many advertising tabloids being given away these days it has the supreme advantage – for me, at least – of coming absolutely free! For several years now this has formed the basis of my hutch floor-covering, but of course needs to be covered with something else.

PEAT has often been suggested, if only for its beneficial effect on the resultant manure. Those who have tried it report that their rabbits seemed to eat it! In any case, it would very quickly stain the rabbits once wet, so cannot be recommended.

CHOPPED STRAW – either oat or barley – is used by many fanciers, over a base of paper, sawdust or shavings. There is no great tendency for the rabbits to eat it, it is quite absorbent and rots down easily. Being absorbent, however, the surface layer will very quickly become wet and I must admit I am reluctant to use it myself, even if it is a lot cheaper than hay.

HAY – good quality meadow hay, that is – was the material I was always taught to use, and I have never doubted its value. Being less absorbent than straw, the urine will quickly percolate down to the newspaper underneath, leaving the surface of the bedding quite dry. It is a very good food, so must be replenished at least once a day to keep an effective thickness in place. I have never experienced any dietary problems caused by the rabbits eating soiled bedding – when it gets dirty they won't eat it, but it must be absolutely free from mildew. There is no finer smell than that of well-made hay – and nothing worse than a mouldy bale, which must on no account be used for any purpose.

CLEANING OUT

A weekly ritual for most fanciers, and those with white rabbits need to do it even more frequently. There can be no doubt that, for show rabbits, very frequent cleaning out is essential, and for these the deep litter of shavings is probably the best.

Dirty bedding will obviously stain a white rabbit very quickly, but it can have just as bad an effect on coloured coats too. Ammonia fumes rising up will soon discolour the belly fur on Rex in general, and Blacks in particular.

As far as other stock is concerned, I am by no means convinced that such regular cleaning is either necessary or even advisable. Consider the doe with a litter: she should not be disturbed from the week before kindling until the young have completely finished with the nest. This can easily mean that her hutch is not completely cleaned out for five weeks or more, with no obvious ill effects.

Watch the reaction of your stud bucks when they are cleaned out: from being placid and content in their surroundings they become restless and irritable until they have succeeded in rearranging and soiling the bedding until it gets to the state they want it. It seems that, by cleaning the hutch out, we have interfered with their territorial instincts, and they will very often not even look at a doe for several days after cleaning out.

I knew several old fanciers who would never clean out a stock hutch until the rabbit's head was touching the roof! Whilst that is too extreme, I have certainly found that my stock are perfectly happy and healthy if their quarters are left undisturbed for several weeks. A daily addition of hay keeps the surface dry and the droppings buried. The underneath layers will slowly ferment, keeping the hutch warm, and not until they become saturated will that hutch be cleaned out.

Mind you, when that does take place, it is a long process, and the manure heap grows at an alarming rate, but to clean out on a weekly basis for non-show stock is, I have come to believe, wasteful and unnecessary.

FEEDING AND HEALTH

CORRECT NUTRITION is, without any doubt, the basis of all 'stockmanship', whether we are considering rabbits or racehorses. John Sandford's *The Domestic Rabbit* devotes some ten thousand words to the subject; it is very tempting to dismiss the subject today with just the one word - pellets!

Our forefathers would have had to devote hours to growing, gathering and/or buying the properly balanced diet which we are lucky enough today to be able to achieve in minutes, at not too great an expense.

Modern pellets and mixes provide a ration which contains all the required major nutrients and trace elements, available all the year round, with no waste and no fear of contamination. Coupled with an adequate supply of water and hay, pellets give us the ability to keep all our stock in optimum condition, and many successful exhibitors use nothing else, but one or two words of warning are needed.

Pelleted feeds were primarily formulated to meet the needs of the commercial meat producer, who required his youngsters to grow to marketable weight as quickly as possible – generally in eight to twelve weeks – without laying down too much fat.

This 'body-building' process requires a large amount of protein, both for the pregnant and suckling doe, and for the weaned youngsters; commercial rabbit pellets, which generally have a protein content of between fifteen and twenty percent, fulfil this requirement admirably. If we ensure that, from about the fourteenth day of pregnancy, our breeding does have constant access to pellets/mixes, water and hay, and we provide the same liberal diet to youngsters up to the age of twelve to fourteen weeks, we will be giving them a first-class start to life.

Beyond that age, however, we have to be a little more circumspect. The rate of growth, whatever the food intake, is lower, and so is the protein requirement. Ad-lib feeding of pellets beyond the age of fourteen weeks is not only wasteful, but may actually cause harm. Excess protein has been shown to result in skin irritation, causing the rabbit to scratch itself and ruin its show prospects. Even if this does not happen, the surplus protein will be converted into energy, and the carbohydrates and oils in the diet – which should fulfil this purpose – will be converted into fat. This will not only spoil the rabbit's type, but may well impair its ability to breed.

There is a considerable body of evidence to suggest that the healthiest and longest-lived animals in other species are those which have had a relatively slow growth in their youth, and I have good reason to suspect that the same applies to Rex rabbits. Youngsters which have been specially nurtured for show and given as many pellets as they will eat will certainly attain size, but rarely achieve that 'hard' condition which is the hallmark of a good exhibition rabbit, and often prove very difficult to breed from. Their siblings which have been retained purely for breeding, and fed a more restricted diet, are, by contrast, much slower to reach maturity, but when they do so they have attained just the same size but are much fitter.

It is therefore true to say that, whilst pellets and mixes have made life much easier for us, they have in no way supplanted stockmanship. The 'poor doers' will obviously have been discarded long before they get to fourteen weeks, but those which are retained must really have individual attention, as just a slight adjustment to the diet can make all the difference between thriving and merely surviving.

In practical terms, it will probably be found necessary to feed between four and six ounces of pellets to newly-weaned stock, and gradually reduce this to about half by the time they are full adults. Every animal is an individual, and has an individual appetite which must be attended to if it is to achieve its full potential: other things being equal, the rabbit which achieves the same growth rate as its litter-mates on a smaller ration of pellets is obviously the one to breed from, and you will almost invariably find that this is the one with the greatest appetite for hay.

THE USE OF HAY

We have already discussed this invaluable substance as a bedding material, but it has an even greater value than that. Prior to the development of pellets, it was usually the case that the fancier with the best oats and hay had the fittest rabbits. We no longer need to

worry about the oats, but it is certainly true that the condition of our stock depends to a very great extend on the quality and quantity of the hay we provide.

Bearing in mind that we have to reduce the pellet intake as the rabbit approaches puberty, the bulk of its food will come from the hay, a constant supply of which should always be available. The best is that harvested in June or early July, before it has shed its seeds and become too fibrous. In some parts of the country clover hay is available as an alternative to the normal meadow hay, and this has an even better feeding value.

Good hay has a very distinctive aroma, and a slight green tinge. Avoid anything which has a dark brown tinge to it, has a musty smell or is obviously mildewed; this has been harvested and cured wet, and will cause untold problems. New hay, before it is about three months old, can also be responsible for scours, so always make sure of adequate last years' stocks between June and September.

A good quality hay, with water, will supply almost all the dietary needs of resting adult stock, which could survive for many weeks on such rations in an emergency. It is very sound practice to provide such a diet, as a matter of course, to potential breeding stock a week or so before mating, to reduce the chance of excess internal fat affecting the productive system.

OTHER FOODS

Whilst pellets, hay and water should always supply the staple diet, other, more traditional foods, as and when available, can be used to advantage. They may not add any nutrients which are not already contained in the pellets and hay, but are useful to provide variety if nothing else. Even a human being might eventually tire of an unremitting diet of best fillet steak – the chance would be a fine thing!

In Spring-time many wild plants – dandelion, sow-thistle, hedge parsley and the like – will be much appreciated, if fed in moderation, and will give a boost to the vitamin intake. Do make sure that you know exactly what plants you are feeding – if you don't know the difference between hedge parsley and hemlock, stick to the pellets! Never feed any wild plants which may have been sprayed, or contaminated by dogs.

Most vegetables used in the home will provide trimmings which can be fed – cauliflower leaves are particularly valuable. Lettuce and cabbage, contrary to popular belief, have little or no nutritional value, and are very prone to cause stomach upsets, so should be avoided. Cooked potatoes can be given, but raw ones, and raw peelings, are supposed to be poisonous. I say supposed, because I once had a cross-bred pet whose absolute favourite foods were raw potatoes and garden bindweed; I could almost guarantee that if I fed such a ration to any of my present stock they would be dead inside a week – but he lived to the ripe old age of thirteen!

It is hardly worthwhile allocating much garden space to vegetables for the rabbits, although I always like to grow some Witloof chicory and a row or two of carrots. The stock seem to appreciate a few chicory leaves above all else, it seems to act as a tonic and conditioner and is often invaluable if a rabbit is unwell and will eat nothing else.

Carrots, I was once told, are the ideal food to keep the colour in Oranges and Castors; dismissed at the time as yet another old-wives' tale to go with the one that rabbits won't drink water, it now appears that there may be some truth in the theory. If the rabbit has a shortage of vitamin D in its diet, it can synthesise it from the carotene pigment in the fur and bloodstream; it is, of course, this pigment which produces the orange colour in the fur, and which is present in high proportions in the carrot!

Many fanciers still use linseed and/or sunflower seeds, even peanuts which they feel give an added gloss to the coat of exhibition stock. Many pellets contain groundnut meal as a source of protein and oils anyway, so it is doubtful if peanuts will achieve anything which a few extra pellets would not.

Sunflower seeds will be eaten by some stock, but not all, but I have never noticed that those which will take them look any fitter than the rest. A mash containing a high proportion of boiled linseed was the classic diet to help a rabbit through the moult; whether it actually did so is a moot point. Certainly a rabbit in heavy moult can utilise extra oils, but it also needs added proteins, so an increase in the pellet ration is probably just as good. Raw linseed can be added to the feed in small quantities, and many very successful exhibitors swear by it; try just a little by all means, but not too much. Raw linseed reacts in the stomach to produce a small quantity of prussic acid, which is not the ideal diet to say the least!

Probably the most under-rated additive to the rations is bread, dried in a slow oven until crisp and golden brown. The rabbits love it, and there are not many households which cannot keep up a fairly constant supply of stale bread. No doubt the 'food-police' will tell us that, as for humans, wholemeal is infinitely superior to white, but the rabbits seem to prefer the latter - and so do I!

UTENSILS

It is quite possible to make or buy quite elaborate food-hoppers and automatic watering systems. It is equally possible - and much cheaper - to make open pots from margarine tubs and the like, embedded in concrete. These take up little floor space and are much less liable to breakage than the crockery pots which the pet shops sell.

Water can be given either in open pots, Ezi-filla top-fill drinkers or standard bottle drinkers, fitted with a metal stem and ball-valve. I have tried these, but with only limited success. Many rabbits never seem to learn how to use them; those that do invariably chew the valve so that it either blocks up completely, or else leaks the contents of the bottle all over the hutch floor. As there is always a problem with algae forming inside the bottles, I have reverted to the open pots, which can at least be easily washed out when dirty.

THE REX, IN SICKNESS AND IN HEALTH

Unlike the original imports, the Rex of today is as healthy as any other breed of rabbit, and I do not propose to discuss common ailments, the diagnosis and treatment of which are adequately covered elsewhere (see Recommended Reading).

SORE HOCKS. With luck, this is the only health problem which the rex fancier is likely to encounter at all regularly. The prevention is very often in the breeding: a very fine coat, completely devoid of guard hairs, will obviously soon wear down to the skin, particularly if the rabbit is too fine in the bone structure. If you look at the back foot of a fine-boned rex, it will appear almost circular in cross-section, whereas a slightly heavier bone will result in a foot which is more semi-circular in shape, with the flat portion towards the bottom. This is obviously a more efficient load-carrier, and a rabbit with this bone-structure, coupled with the correct coat texture, should keep fur on its feet throughout its show life.

With increasing age, the tendency for the feet to lose their covering also increases; it is probable that most of our breeding stock has bare hocks to a certain extent. Within limits, this must be accepted, and does not appear to affect the rabbit. Kept in contact with a bare floor, or saturated bedding, however, and the skin will very quickly become inflamed and bleed, and then the rabbit will certainly suffer.

Very often the first sign of trouble is seen when the animal is continuously shaking its front feet in obvious discomfort. The first step is to provide soft, dry bedding, then to thoroughly clean and disinfect the affected feet. Various antiseptic creams are available in the pet shops,

Ermine Rex with sore hocks

but are often a general purpose type of ointment which will do no harm – but not much good either.

The one certain cure I have found is a product called 'Vetsovate'; this is obviously a derivative of a cream used for the treatment of dermatitis in human beings, and really works. Gently rubbed in to the affected parts twice daily, the inflammation will disappear in two to three days, and within a week, the fur should be growing again. The one snag is that it is only available on prescription, so you will have to get it from the vet.

FIRST STEPS

TO THE EXPERIENCED FANCIER, who merely wishes to widen his interests in a different breed, obtaining foundation stock should present little difficulty, it being a merely a question of which friend or acquaintance to approach.

The novice has no such advantage: the choice of colours in the Rex may be bewildering; he will have little idea whether what appears a good choice on paper will prove satisfactory in practice; he may not even have ever attended a rabbit show as a potential new fancier. The next few paragraphs are directed primarily at just such a novice: the more experienced will, I hope, bear with me, remembering that we all had to make a start somewhere.

The first step for the complete novice must be to find out about rabbit clubs within easy reach of home. Even in these days when more and more local clubs are curtailing their activities, it is usually possible to attend at least one show every weekend without travelling much more than thirty miles. All open shows advertise in the *RABBITS* supplement of *Fur & Feather* and, whilst there may be little point at this stage in becoming a member of the British Rabbit Council, they are only too pleased to send an information pack to any prospective recruit, which will tell you a great deal about the rudiments of this fascinating hobby.

When you attend your first show, try not to be a "wallflower". You are there to learn, which you won't do if you sit in a corner and talk to nobody. Whilst it is definitely not a good idea to try to button-hole an obviously busy official – or even the judge whilst he's working! – there is always a lot of activity near the judging tables. Find out where the Rex are to be judged, and join the crowd! With very few exceptions, the Rex fanciers are only too willing to welcome a novice into their midst, and almost certainly you will soon find yourself involved in stewarding.

If you are not very accustomed to handling rabbits, don't be afraid to say so, and you will soon be shown the correct way to handle a rabbit on the table, even if you lack the confidence to take it from its pen. Bear in mind that a great deal of effort has been put into preparing these exhibits for show, and they must be treated with due respect.

Assuming that there is a representative selection of Rex at the show, you will soon be able to relate the mental picture this book has tried to give you, with the actual animal in the flesh. It may prove that stock in the variety you think you would like to keep is actually present at the show, and does well. In such a case, you might be tempted to approach the owner and make him an offer which he can't afford to refuse. My advice would be -"Festina Lente" - make haste slowly. Have a good talk to as many people as you can, to make sure that you would get a fair deal, and that the breed in question is really right for you.

What is the best Rex variety for the novice? There are almost as many opinions on this as there are varieties, so much depends on what you really want from your hobby. If your ambition runs to being B.I.S. every time you show, then you will obviously go for Ermines, Blacks or Seals which are statistically the most successful colours. Remember, though, that competition within these colours is generally stronger and prices higher; also, your lack of experience will hamper your preparation of stock in the early days, and that your expensive purchase may be marked down because it has not been presented at its best.

Nevertheless, I would hesitate to discourage anyone from keeping these breeds but, particularly in the case of the Ermine, a lot of outside assistance is going to be needed in the matter of learning how to put a rabbit down in good show condition.

There are some breeds where it is almost impossible to buy stock from the leading exhibitors. Fortunately, this rarely applies to the Rex, although there is always the odd breeder who will never sell anything which has the slightest chance of beating him in the future. If you have taken my advice about making discreet inquiries, you will avoid this type. The thinking fancier will be only too pleased to be beaten – occasionally – by stock which he has supplied: it can only enhance his reputation for fair dealing.

Many people find more satisfaction in the less popular colours, many of which offer a great deal of interest in watching their development from nest to adulthood. They may not have the reputation of world-beaters, which is not to say that a dedicated and scientific breeder could not make them so. I would, however, have to discourage the absolute novice from trying a really rare colour like the Opal or Cinnamon as his first choice; not only is stock in extremely short supply, but the majority of judges see so few of them that even a very good one is liable to be overlooked.

Whether or not you manage to locate a suitable source of foundation stock from your first few visits to a show will, then, depend largely on your chosen variety. If it just is not available reasonably close to home, it is a very good idea to buy a Rex of any colour and show it, purely to gain the experience – and widen your circle of friends – until such time as your first choice becomes available.

THE CHOICE OF FOUNDATION STOCK

Your initial foray into the exhibition world has now located a source for your first rabbits. Depending upon the breed, you will either have a very wide choice, or none at all.

The most consistent rex winners are (top to bottom) Ermine, Black, Siamese Seal

It could well happen that, if you are determined to have a very rare variety, there is only one breeder in the country with anything at all to sell, in which case it is Hobson's choice. You must take what is on offer, pay the asking price or choose another variety.

If you have a choice, you must now decide whether to go to two or even more breeders, or get everything you want from the one source. You must also decide whether to buy young stock to show, and then breed from; mature stock not suitable for showing but capable of breeding winners; or adult show rabbits capable of winning straight away, and then being bred from. To a very large degree, your bank balance will make the decision for you!

SOURCES

The fancier of experience might look at what is available, and think along these lines: breeder A has stock of good coat and colour, but I don't like his type; breeder B offers better type, good colour but not quite the coat of A, whilst breeder C has both type and coat even though there is a slight failing on colour. Obviously, all the genes for near perfection exist within those three strains, so if I buy stock from all three, I can establish my own strain which will beat them all.

The logic cannot be faulted: with sufficient determination and skill, those genes for excellence must be capable of being combined into one rabbit. On the other hand, they might well be recessive genes which will be masked once the three strains are combined; the first litters would appear to be absolute rubbish. This is very much a long-term task, only to be undertaken by someone with a great deal of patience, and hutch space. Because of the extremely large gene-pool, practically all of the F1 generation would have to be kept and bred from before any meaningful selection could be undertaken. Given the necessary space, and the ability to wait probably three years to see any results from one's labours, this is a very sound plan, but it is not for the novice.

He is much better advised to follow the time-honoured course of buying stock from just the one breeder, and preferably one who can truly claim to have his own strain. By this, we mean one who produces stock to a consistent pattern which, even if it falls short of perfection in some aspects, can be relied upon to replicate itself from generation to generation.

If you have such a breeder locally, so much the better. If your nearest source can only turn out one or two good rabbits a year, together with a lot of rubbish, it is better to go further afield. This man obviously is not breeding selectively to a plan, and his good rabbits are no better than flukes.

WHAT TO BUY

It is obviously tempting, if the pocket will permit it, to go out and buy a trio of winners in the hope that, by so doing, you will start at the top and stay there. Whilst this does occasionally happen, the more usual result is disappointment. What very often happens is that the rabbit which has been shown a great deal has put on so much fat that its ability to breed is impaired – sometimes permanently. At best, this can mean a long wait until breeding condition is reached, and even then it will probably be found that, although all three rabbits had won, they all suffered from one tiny fault which will appear as a much bigger fault in all their offspring. If the stock is still capable of winning, you will obviously be expected to pay a high price, and in the long run it may just not be worth it.

Experience tells us that most big winners come from the mating of balanced pairs; a buck which excels where the doe may fail slightly, and vice-versa. Whilst they may – indeed must – not suffer from any major fault, they are not in themselves capable of competing at the highest level.

YOUNG STOCK

A little calculation will show us that by the time a rabbit has reached seven months of age, it will have consumed at least £12 worth of pellets at 2003 prices. Add to that the cost of hay, bedding, wear and tear of equipment, etc., and it is obvious that even pet-shop quality adults cannot be sold at less than £20 without the breeder showing a loss. To adequately compensate himself for the years of dedicated and skilful breeding, his subscriptions to various bodies, and the thousands of miles travelled to shows, he ought to charge at least twice that for stock of good breeding potential, even more if it is still showable. We should be so lucky! Whilst there will always be the odd breeder with a very high reputation who will ask that sort of price, and the odd newcomer who is prepared to pay it, the majority of fanciers prefer to buy and sell at a much earlier age. At twelve to fourteen weeks, we can usually tell whether the youngster has good potential. If bought at an earlier age, it is more difficult to assess the quality, and this should be reflected in a lower price. In any case, it should always be possible to buy two promising youngsters for the price of one mature adult.

ADULT STOCK

Here, we are not talking about winners, but purely breeding stock. Those which, for some reason or other have never been seriously shown, but have been retained by the breeder either to sell or to use himself. If we are to be strictly logical, a doe of this type, suitably mated, should cost us more than its litter sister which has become a Champion, but logic does not seem to extend that far in any branch of livestock breeding. Two mated does could provide a very sound start, to be returned to the original breeder for re-mating once the first litter has been weaned. From the four litters we should be able to select enough young does to show and to provide future breeding stock.

It is very doubtful if it is worth retaining any bucks at this stage, unless one is particularly outstanding. A buck suitable for stud purposes will not be a good proposition for showing, and in a very small stud will not be used often enough to ensure he is always fertile. Within very wide limits, it has been conclusively proved that, the more often the male is used, the more sperm he produces, and the higher its quality.

Provided that your original supplier is reasonably close at hand, it is much better to return the does to him for mating until you can justify keeping a stud buck yourself.

By far the best type of foundation stock is the proven breeder: the doe which has already demonstrated that she can rear a good sized litter of quality youngsters. Such a doe should be able to continue doing so for about three years, and is worth her weight in gold – which is what the breeder will probably ask for! To buy a doe more than three years old is a speculation rather than an investment: you may get one, even two more litters from her, equally she may be barren.

The novice who has taken pains to cultivate friendships in the right quarters may well be able to obtain proven breeders, at a price which reflects that friendship. Otherwise, such stock is beyond the reach of most of us, and a young mated doe or two will have to suffice, or some youngsters for growing on. The higher the risk, the lower the price.

As a final thought on this topic, never disdain stock which is advertised in the Fancy Press and, in later years, make use of this medium for your own surplus stock. If selling, never offer anything you would not keep yourself if you had the room. If buying, make sure that any claims as to the quality of the stock can be validated, preferably by an independent opinion. It is quite possible to register a Champion which has never actually met another rabbit in competition; it only requires five rather reluctant signatures to a Challenge Certificate. If the vendor will not agree to inspection by a mutually agreed authority before the sale is finalised, it is better to look elsewhere.

QUARANTINE

Whatever type of stock you buy, and wherever it comes from, it is simply asking for trouble to put it all in the same building, together with any stock you may already have. A few outdoor hutches are invaluable for quarantine purposes, and to isolate any stock which is suspected to be unhealthy. Newly obtained stock should always be fed and handled last, for at least three weeks, by which time any hidden diseases should have become apparent.

FEEDING

Always find out what the previous owner fed, and at what times, and maintain that system for the first few days, after which you can begin to get the new stock gradually accustomed to your own regime. Whilst a drastic change in diet can have a bad effect, particularly on young stock, it is probably true that a change in meal-times will be even worse. The rabbit is a crepuscular animal, i.e. it is most active around dawn and dusk, and the closer to those two periods we can feed our stock, the better.

Provided that hay and water is always available, concentrates only need to be given once a day. Whether you give these in the morning, and top-up water and hay in the evening, or the other way round, really does not matter, as long as you are consistent. Feeding times should never vary by more than two hours, otherwise there is a danger that the rabbit will get too hungry and gorge itself when the food does eventually arrive.

Does with litters, and youngsters up to about fourteen weeks of age, should always have a supply of pellets in front of them, so their pots will almost certainly need to be filled twice a day, or even more frequently. Whilst it is possible to specify a certain amount of food as a basic ration, this can only really be treated as a rule of thumb; good stockmanship depends on one's powers of observation, ensuring that each animal is fed according to its needs, which will not always match up to what the text-books say. The needs, of course, will vary according to the time of year, the rabbit's development and its level of activity. It is often possible that once-daily attention will suffice, but if the rabbit needs caring for three times a day, then that is what it must get if it is to realise its full potential.

Good observation will soon show up the poor performers – those which eat twice as much as the one in the next hutch yet are not bigger or fitter. They may be diseased, they may be infected with worms or other parasites, or they may have a genetic inferiority. If the possibility of disease or parasites can be ruled out, then this is the sort of animal NOT to be bred from, however good its other properties.

BREEDING
The expression "they breed like rabbits" was definitely not coined by a rabbit fancier. Generally speaking, the average fancier has far more difficulty in getting his does into kindle when he wants them to be, than he does in controlling a population explosion! Whilst the Rex is no worse – or better – than other breeds in this respect, it is perhaps worthwhile looking at the reproductive cycle in some detail: some failures may be due to inherited tendencies which are part and parcel of domestication, but others are more likely to be due to our own failure to take into account the rabbit's natural life-cycle.

In the wild, young rabbits can generally be found as early as

February, with a more or less constant rate of production up to October, after which few, if any, litters are born. In Winter, of course, food supplies are so restricted that any young born could not be expected to survive, but this is not the basic reason for the break in reproduction: the rabbits do not make a conscious decision not to breed, but they are very much influenced by the lack of daylight at this time of year.

It has been firmly established that the breeding cycle, in both bucks and docs, is controlled by hormones which are produced in the pituitary gland. To an extent, the activity of the gland is genetically controlled, but it is very much influenced by the amount of daylight available. It has been found that during Winter the production of hormones is very low indeed until the slight lengthening of daylight hours which occurs in the new year. Whilst the increase in daylight is scarcely noticeable to us, it appears to act as a trigger to the pituitary gland, and, over a period of just a few weeks, hormone production rises to a peak. It stays more or less constant throughout the Summer, and then falls off dramatically after the September equinox.

Whilst it may seem strange that a rabbit, which spends so much of its life underground, should be so influenced by the daylight it sees so little of, it is a fact, and, of course, it ensures that most litters will be born at the time of maximum food availability. Thus, the old-fashioned idea in many areas of stock-breeding, that pairing up should take place on St Valentine's Day, is not very wide of the mark.

It has also been found, in the wild, that the earliest litters are born to the youngest does, those bred towards the end of the previous season. What has never been properly established, of course, is the number of matings in the wild which do not result in a litter; it may well be that the number of "misses" is just as high in Nature as it is in our rabbitries, but we can at least learn one or two lessons from the wild.

Firstly, we are no longer dependant upon seasonal food supplies, and can thus expect to be able to rear a litter at any time of year. However, if we want this to be between September and February, we have got to give our stock artificial light to keep up the supply of hormones. Since the pituitary also produces the growth hormones, it is obvious that extra light is also necessary to ensure that the youngsters thrive. Whether artificial light is really adequate for the full production of growth hormones is open to question; however well they are cared for, winter-bred stock invariably takes longer to mature than that born during the natural season.

Secondly, it is very much to be doubted that the practice of allowing our does to reach full maturity before mating is a sound one. Whilst the Rex, being that much bigger than a wild rabbit, could hardly be expected to reach full sexual maturity at five months, there seems little doubt that we would suffer fewer "misses" if we mated our does before they quite reach full adulthood and have laid down a lot of fat around the ovaries.

This is another good reason for not breeding from stock which has had a long show career: in the long run, it may well pay to "breed from the best, and show the rest" as has been advised in other fancies. Certainly, the doe which has been allowed to develop at a steady rate until it is about six months old is likely to prove far more ready to breed than her sister, fed maximum rations and shown until the age of seven or eight months. Inevitably, she will need several weeks of strict dieting to get down to breeding condition, by which time her sister should be rearing her second litter!

Another fallacy is to allow a long resting period between litters. A doe will achieve her maximum milk production about three weeks after kindling, after which it falls off quite rapidly. She could, with advantage, be remated after the sixth week without detriment to her current or future litter. If weaning is delayed until the eighth week or beyond, and the doe then rested for a few more weeks, the usual consequence is the laying down of fat and difficulty in remating.

PSEUDO-PREGNANCY

This is a very common condition observed in many animals, and, as far as the rabbit is concerned, is probably the cause of the majority of missed matings. Reacting to stimulus, which may be a mounting by a buck, or even normal handling by the owner, the doe sheds her eggs and begins to produce hormones to maintain a pregnancy. This means that she cannot possible conceive, however often she is mated, whilst the condition persists. After about sixteen days, the production of these hormones would be taken over by the placenta had the doe been subject to a fertile mating; however, since the eggs were not fertilised, the doe is not actually pregnant, she just thinks she is! Without the placenta, hormone production ceases, and the doe thinks she is about to give birth – so she makes a nest, even though there is nothing to put into it!

This is a source of great frustration to the fancier in two ways. A litter may have been planned to be five months old at a certain date, which will now be missed. Equally, there may have been no plans for a litter at all, but the doe pulls the fur from her chest two days before the show at which she might have gained her championship! The cause is the same in both cases: the doe has no fixed sexual cycle, and can shed her eggs almost at will, in response to a stimulus which may be no more than being groomed. For a period of about three weeks the doe will look and behave as if she is pregnant, but is not, and cannot possibly become so.

Since there is nothing the fancier can do to overcome the situation, all he can do is to salvage the one crumb of comfort which exists. At the termination of a pseudo-pregnancy, the doe is at her most fertile, and a mating now will almost certainly result in a proper pregnancy. I have now made it an invariable habit to remate my does between eighteen and twentyone days after the first mating; if she is actually pregnant, she will probably refuse to mate again, and even if she does, no harm will be done to the embryos. If she was in pseudo-pregnancy then the second mating will almost invariably produce youngsters – if the buck is fertile.

THE STUD BUCK

As has already been said, the buck needs as good a diet as the expectant doe, and to be given plenty of work. He is also just as much at the mercy of his pituitary gland so that, although he may appear to be performing as well as normal in Winter, his actual sperm count may be so low as to preclude a successful pregnancy for the doe. He will also tend to be less fertile if in heavy moult – and in any case no rabbit should be bred from, buck or doe, if in full moult. Not that this will automatically ensure that their offspring will be in perpetual moult, as the old saying has it. The inability to moult quickly and cleanly has many causes, some genetic, some due to mis-management. If the parent stock normally clear the moult quickly, they should pass on this characteristic to their offspring; if, however, both parents are in heavy moult at the time of mating, the buck may well be sterile. Even if he is not, the extra strain of mating on top of moulting may well delay its completion, whilst as far as the doe is concerned she has to contend with the strain of moulting as well as providing for the coming litter, to the ultimate detriment of both.

Unless the buck is in practically constant use – say every other day – it is as well to treat the first mating as potentially sterile, and return the doe to him after a rest of two or three minutes (I hope it should not be necessary to emphasise that the doe should always be put into the buck's hutch, and not vice-versa).

The two acts of mating should ensure that the doe will shed her eggs, but occasionally there may be a delay, or eggs may be released from only one of the ovaries. Since the sperm is only active for a relatively short time, it is often advised that the doe be remated four to six hours after the first time – a case of belt and braces. Personally, I have never found that doing so did anything to reduce the number of misses, in fact most does are very reluctant to mate again after so short an interval. There is nothing to be lost – other than extra wear and tear on the buck – by repeat matings after twenty-four hours, if the doe is willing.

DIFFICULT MATINGS

So far, we have been discussing the frustration caused by apparently good matings failing to result in any offspring. What can be equally annoying is when the two animals positively refuse to mate; this can have a number of causes, mainly the fault of the doe.

An experienced stud buck, in good but not fat condition, should attempt to mate any doe with no encouragement; if he will not try, he is probably unwell in some way, and the cause must be eliminated before any further attempts are made. A young buck, put with a receptive doe, will very soon learn what is expected of him.

If the doe is more than usually reluctant to mate, and particularly if she becomes aggressive, she should be removed immediately, otherwise that buck is going to become discouraged from stud duties for a long time to come.

Almost invariably, though, the reluctance to mate will be on the doe's part. She may be too old or too young to breed; she may be too fat or too thin; it may be too early or too late in the year; or she may be pseudo-pregnant, in which case an attempted mating every other day will eventually solve the problem. Extra light ought to help with out-of-season breeding, and should really have been used for several weeks before the attempted mating.

Generally speaking, though, most does which are reluctant to mate have been allowed to become too fat.

This is the major reason why the best show animals rarely make the best mothers – there is a big difference between show condition and breeding condition. A good layer of fat on the back of the rabbit is necessary for the show bench, but unfortunately this is usually the last place a doe will lay down her reserves. The first fat is invariably deposited round the kidneys, the next layer will be around the ovaries and only then will body fat begin to accumulate. Thus, long before the doe is fully fit for show, she is likely to have laid down such an amount of internal fat that the reproductive organs cannot function properly.

The cure for this condition is drastic – in fact if the doe is over a year old there may be no cure at all, the damage is probably permanent. Younger than that, a very drastic reduction in her rations is the only answer; there must be no oils or fat in the diet, just sufficient protein for cell renewal, and less carbohydrate than she actually requires for her normal energy production. She will be forced to draw on her fat reserves literally to stay alive, and she will not begin to use up the fat around the ovaries until all the body fat has gone. A rabbit can live on nothing but hay and water for a very long time, and this is all she must be allowed. A little fresh green-food will not come terribly amiss, but cereals and concentrates are absolutely taboo.

At the end of this enforced starvation period, the doe will not be fat, and neither will she be fit, as she will inevitably have lost some muscle tissue as well as the fat. She must therefore be put back onto normal maintenance rations for a week or two before she is mated. By then, she will be in rising condition, and if she will not breed now, she never will.

Very occasionally, a pair of rabbits can be mated time after time, with no result. The only solution then is to mate them to different, proven, partners. As a pair, they must carry lethal genes which prevent the fertilisation of the ova, or cause the embryos to die early in their development. If this happens in your stud, a very careful watch must be kept since, even if they produce young with a different mate, that lethal gene will have been transmitted to their offspring.

CARE OF THE BROOD DOE

Assuming that the doe has mated successfully, what extra care now needs to be given? For the first two weeks, none at all; at this stage of the embryo's development, the doe will have adequate resources to feed them. Extra rations will only be used to form fat which could cause difficulty in kindling; furthermore, she may be pseudo-pregnant or not pregnant at all, in which case the extra fat will impair future matings.

There are some fanciers who claim to be able to tell, twelve days after mating, whether or not the doe is in kindle. This is done by palpating the abdomen, when the embryos can be felt as a row of marbles just in front of the groin. Even to the practised hand, it is not an infallible method. If there are only one or two embryos they can easily be missed, or faecal pellets may be mistaken for embryos. Most importantly, the embryos can be fatally damaged by an inexperienced hand; it is not a technique at which I can claim a proficiency, and I would only advise its use under the strict supervision of someone who has learned to use it safely and effectively.

After the fourteenth day, the rations can safely be increased by up to fifty percent, and the doe remated on or about the twenty-first day – sooner if there is any sign of nest-building; this will guard against a possible pseudo-pregnancy. After that time, the doe can have up to double her normal rations, and if she now starts to build a nest, it will be in earnest. Many experienced does will start to make a nest a week or more before the litter is due, whilst others believe in waiting until the very last moment.

Kindling

Depending on the size of the litter, the birth will occur between

twenty-eight and thirty-five days after mating, and the doe will very often go off her food for a day or two before kindling; this is usually a good sign that something is about to happen! The normal interval between mating and kindling is thirty-two days, although I have known does to go as much as a week beyond this with a very small litter. One, at least, will be born dead, and will have been the obvious cause of the delay. If the doe is in obvious distress, a vet should be consulted; he may well be able to save the doe, if not her babies.

In the majority of cases, the litter will be born at night and placed into the previously constructed nest. Sometimes, particularly with a maiden doe, the nest is not made until after the birth, with the result that some or all of the babies will be found chilled on the floor of the hutch the next morning. In many cases they can be revived by holding their bodies in warm water. They can then be returned very carefully to the nest, but not before the scent of humans has been removed.

This is a precaution which must be taken whenever very young rabbits are handled and, distasteful as it may seem to some, the best way of doing it is to rub the hands in the doe's droppings. She should, of course, be removed from the hutch whilst the nest is being disturbed, and not returned until the babies have properly settled.

It is all too common to find a doe's first litter scattered, possibly mutilated, and beyond recovery. She should be remated immediately, and will usually have developed the full maternal instinct by the time she kindles again.

If she should scatter the next litter, then I would not use her again.

Normally, though, the doe will have put the babies into the nest and cleaned up the after-birth long before the owner is awake. There is nothing to gain, and much to lose, by disturbing the nest at this stage. It should not be examined until the third or fourth day, and then only to remove any obvious runts or deformities. If there are more than eight babies, and a smaller litter available into which some might be fostered, then this can be done - always assuming the owner will be able to tell later which offspring belongs to which doe. Any form of artificial marking at this stage is fraught with danger, and should not be attempted.

Generally speaking, the doe knows what is best, and should be left to get on with it. The object of this particular stage of the exercise is to get the youngsters thriving, and the longer they stay in the nest, on a diet of the richest milk of any small mammal, the better they will be. The more they are handled, the more likely they are to leave the nest too soon.

Ideally, the babies will stay put until they are about three weeks old, by which time most varieties will be giving some indication of their potential. Type should show a distinct cobbiness, with bold head even in does, and nice short ears. Any which look at all dubious at this stage are almost certain to fail as adults.

Although the colour will be several shades lighter than it will be eventually, it should certainly be possible to pick out the best. Indeed, with the agouti varieties, this is probably the best time to assess their definition; although many Chinrex will have a distinct brown cast to the pearling, the demarcation between that and the base should be clearly visible, whilst the other agoutis should be an almost perfect miniature of an adult, except for a much lighter top. Although the rabbit will not actually begin to moult out of its nest or baby coat until about the sixth week, it is noticeable that the pigment begins to fade before this, so there is not much time to make one's assessment.

Coat quality is by no means easy to determine at this stage; a well-fed baby will always feel dense, it may well carry guard hairs and some curl which will moult out in the next coat, so all one can really do at this stage is to determine the really long-coated ones.

Unfortunately, the Rex does not develop at a regular rate, and what looks like a potential world-beater at four weeks of age will probably look like a pet-shop reject the next week! It is therefore very wise to mark the most promising babies as soon as they are spotted, and at this age they are much too young for a B.R.C. ring. A spot of vegetable-based dye on the inner ear, or a felt-tipped pen will give sufficient identification until a ring can be fitted.

Whilst excessive length of coat, body or ears are faults which are unlikely to improve with age, many other apparent shortcomings may well do so. The sorting of stock in the baby coat is done, not so much as to select the best, but to eliminate the obvious misfit. The majority of the youngsters will have to be kept for several months before a proper assessment can be made, and many an ugly duckling has grown up into a swan.

WEANING

Opinions differ greatly as to the best age to wean the youngsters; they are quite capable of surviving should they lose their mother when they are a mere three or four weeks old, but, on the other hand, it is not unknown for two does to stay with their mother until they are full adults. There is no hard and fast rule between these two extremes, and as much depends on the well-being of the doe as that of the youngsters.

The doe's milk production falls off rapidly after the third week, and has normally ceased completely by the end of the sixth week, when it should be safe enough to remove her. Always make a visual check of her teats, though, before you do so and, if there is any doubt, leave her another week. Congestion of the teats is a painful condition, and may result in permanent damage. By far the best way to prevent it is to mate the doe up again.

If the doe is not removed by the end of the eighth week, she will be competing with the youngsters for food. They require a constant supply of pellets – she definitely does not! Somewhere between the sixth and eighth week, then, should be the safest time to wean, and it should be an invariable rule to leave the litter in the hutch in which they were born, and put the doe elsewhere. Although they no longer rely on her for their food, there is always a slight trauma for the youngsters when the doe has gone; if they also have to contend with strange surroundings they will inevitably suffer a set-back to their growth.

GROWING ON

It used to be advised that the youngsters should be separated into individual hutches as soon as possible after weaning, but I am not at all sure that that is the best policy. The rabbit is a social animal until the urge to breed overtakes it, and will thrive much better in company.

This is where the owner's powers of observation must really come into play. Any youngsters which are obviously not worth retaining should be removed by the tenth week, but the others left together until the sex hormones begin to take effect, and the youngsters start to mount each other. Even then, it is not always necessary to use individual hutches. Two does can normally be left together until they are full adults, even two bucks can do so, although in the latter case we usually find that one will quickly establish dominance, to the detriment of the other's growth and coat. Whatever you do, never leave more than two animals of either sex together beyond fourteen weeks; the weakest will inevitable suffer damage, sometimes quite severe.

Stock which is only going to be used for future breeding can be left in pairs for as long as they will continue to live together amicably. There may be the occasional skirmish, which will rarely result in more than a tuft of fur pulled out, but generally they will mature better than they would if separated early. Of course, once they have been mated they will no longer tolerate the presence of another rabbit in their hutch, whatever their sex.

Youngsters which are of show quality will need individual hutches by the fourteenth week, as even the slightly horse-play may result in a bunch of white hairs which will never go away. Do try to make sure, in the arrangement of your rabbitry, that the rabbits can see each other – visual contact is the next best thing to the physical kind.

PREPARATION FOR SHOW

Whether or not you are already an experienced exhibitor, you will begin to assess the show potential of your youngsters from the moment they leave the nest. You will get the most promising ones used to being handled from an early age, and daily handling and light grooming with the hands is all most Rex need in the way of show preparation.

Although we have quite detailed descriptions of what is required, in the standards, the most important attributes of any show animal are the unwritten ones! To succeed, the rabbit must be docile enough to be handled, it must be fit, it must be clean and it must be in full coat. Whilst some Rex are not renowned for their tractability on the judging table, in the vast majority of cases the daily handling and grooming from at least the time of weaning will take care of the docility aspect. The judge wants to see a rabbit sitting boldly and confidently on the table – literally asking to be given first prize. He does not want the one which refuses to stay still, or the one which lies in a cowering heap like a sack of coals. Regular handling is the answer, and the rabbit will soon learn to stand rather than lie on the table.

FITNESS. This is, to a very great extent, an inherited characteristic, in that adults which are easy to maintain in firm flesh and full, glossy coat will usually produce young with the same attributes. A good stockman can often, with almost constant attention, put a semblance of show condition onto a rabbit which otherwise would never be more than half fit, but, in general, we have to breed for fitness before we feed for it.

Naturally, the full potential fitness of the rabbit can only be achieved in the correct environment; plenty of space, fresh air, good bedding and, above all, good feeding. It is no use making a sudden decision to increase the feeding of a three-month old youngster which has had little more than bare subsistence rations: good feeding must start before the rabbit is even conceived.

If the instructions regarding the brood doe have been followed, she will have been fully fit, but not fat, when she was mated, and reared the litter at its optimum rate of growth. Once the babies start to take solid food, the onus begins to be transferred to the owner. From then on, an adequate, balanced diet should enable the rabbit's genes to do their work unimpeded.

"Balanced" is probably the most important word in the previous sentence. A very high protein content is needed in the very early days, but this must be gradually reduced from about three months in favour of fibre and carbohydrates. Adequate space is needed to exercise and firm up the muscles, otherwise the food will be converted into fat and not flesh. Whilst a layer of fat in the right places is essential to fill out the finished rabbit, the flesh must be there first.

Whilst the basic diet of pellets, hay and water will keep the rabbit at about ninetyfive percent of its full potential fitness, it may be necessary for a few additives to be given to add the finishing touches. Several suggestions have been made in the chapter on feeding; experimentation on a small scale is the only answer.. What suits one rabbit may well have no effect on another, and a major change to the diet will not have a good effect on any. If the underlying bone structure is correct, it must be obvious even to the novice that a good diet will enable the rabbit to develop good type. What may not be so obvious is that it is also essential for the proper development of coat and colour; neither will be found to their proper advantage if the rabbit is not fit and clean.

CLEANLINESS should go without saying, yet time and again judges find exhibits good enough to win, until they are turned over, when it seems that they must have walked to the show across a ploughed field. To stand any chance of winning, the rabbit must be shown clean, which means that it must be kept clean at all times. Accidental stains can usually be removed if treated early enough, but ingrained dirt is difficult if not impossible to remove without damaging the fur.

Instructions on how to keep a rabbit clean, and to remove minor stains have been given in the chapter on the Ermine, since this is the variety which shows the dirt most. However, all Rex can get dirty – even dust can mar the colour and coat of all breeds. So, while we may well need not worry too much about the frequency at which we clean out our stock hutches, potential show stock must receive special attention almost from the moment they leave the nest.

The biggest enemy is the combination of droppings and urine which, by its acid reaction will irreversibly dye the fur unless it is removed straight away. Sponging with a solution of household detergent will sometimes do the trick, but often more drastic measures will be required. Surgical spirit and witch-hazel are old and trusted stand-bys, whilst in recent years products have come onto the market which are worth trying. Even the dog-fanciers' favourite chalk block will sometimes suffice, as long as no trace of powder is left behind. The same comment applies to the many proprietary powders – even the finely divided magnesia powder used by furriers; they can all be used, provided that no traces remain for the judge to find.

Most exhibitors have their own favourite preparation for general and emergency use. All of them have one thing in common:- they will not touch etched-in stains, which are going to be visible until Nature removes them in the next moult. So, the only valid advice is to keep the rabbit clean, check it every day, and attack any stains as soon as they are spotted, before they have a chance to become permanent.

FULL COAT
This last requirement of show condition is, in a way, wishful thinking. Whilst adult rabbits normally moult the complete coat in Autumn, and may be in full coat for eight or nine months, most Rex will have begun to lose type and colour (or been retired for breeding) before they enter the stage of annual moulting. We are concerned with the intermediate and first adult coats.

The intermediate coat is the one which begins to grow between the fourth and sixth weeks and is usually complete by the five and a half to six month stage. This is almost immediately replaced by the growth of the first adult coat, which may be finished when the rabbit is seven months old, but more usually is not complete for another month or even two. Much depends on the time of year – early bred youngsters may attain their first adult coat in Autumn and immediately break into another moult. Those which reach maturity in Winter may very often keep the first adult coat for six months, although by the end of that period it would look much the worse for wear.

In general, the problem with the Rex is that we show it in the intermediate and first adult coats, which take a long time to produce, and begin to be moulted out almost as soon as they are complete - sometimes even before they are complete. The cynics amongst us will say that the Rex is only in full coat on one weekend in the year, when our partner drags us off to a wedding or – perish the thought

– Christmas shopping!

Having such a dense coat, it will naturally take a Rex longer to complete a moult than any other breed. Whilst a slight lack of finish may affect the rabbit's chances in mixed duplicate classes, within the breed it should not stop us showing, as all will probably be under the same handicap. If we waited for our exhibits to be in perfect coat, there would be no shows! Whilst it is pointless – and unfair to the health of the rabbit – to show it in full moult, when the moult is two-thirds to three-quarters complete it is generally possible to put the rabbit out showing minimal effect of the change of coat, and this means grooming.

Quite elaborate grooming kits – brushes, combs, etc – are much in evidence with other breeds. They are quite unnecessary with the Rex, in fact positively harmful. On the intermediate coat in particular, nothing but the hands should be used. If there is a great deal of dead, loose hair to be removed, the hands may be dampened, but that is all. This coat is very delicate, and will not stand up to being brushed or combed. Grooming should be carried out for a short period every day, rather than being left for a prolonged session the night before a show; the latter practice will result in a great deal of work being done on the coat, from which it will not have time to recover, and will remain 'choppy' and uneven. The final grooming, with dry hands, just before penning the rabbit, will put the final gloss to the finish. You may, if you wish, get a good gloss by polishing with a silk cloth or a chamois grooming glove.

Grooming of the adult coat can be a little more vigorous, but brushes should still not be used. If there is a great deal of dead hair to get out, the coat may be made quite wet rather than damp. It may take up to a week to fully recover from this treatment, so don't leave that job until the last moment. In general, the last places to clear the moult are the nape, chest and rump, just above the tail. Nothing but hand-grooming can be used in the nape, where the fur is usually finer and less dense than normal anyway. Chest and rump can, though, sometimes benefit from a combing.

It will often be found that, in these areas, the dead hair, instead of coming away cleanly, tends to take on a curl and mat into the adjacent coat. A fine-tooth comb will remove this, although we must not be so rough as to pull away fur which is not yet quite ready to leave the skin. This may well damage the follicle, and the next hair to grow there will be curly, possibly white. Some fanciers swear by the use of an old, practically worn-out piece of hack-saw blade to clear dead and curly hair above the tail. I have seen this done in a show-hall, and judging by the pile of fur left on the floor, it was most effective. Since the uneven coat left behind was probably just as noticeable as the moulty patch, I hardly need comment that the job should have been done several days previously.

There is a great deal of mystique sometimes attached to show preparation, but there is really no magic formula. With good feeding, clean housing and daily, gentle, grooming it should be possible to take a Rex from its hutch straight to the show with every hope of success. Do remember, though, to keep the claws regularly clipped, down to about an eighth of an inch from the central blood vessel. Overlong claws spoil the stance, may lead to sore pads, and can damage both the rabbit and the judge, not to mention the stewards.

EXHIBITION STANDARDS

If the reader did not already have that knowledge, I hope the preceding chapters will have enabled him – or her – to set up a rabbitry ready for the introduction of stock. Naturally, the best which can be afforded is the minimum requirement!

What, then, constitutes a good Rex?

As with all forms of exhibition livestock, we must have a standard of excellence which we hope our stock will approach. Some would use the term "standard of perfection", but the "perfect" animal - be it race-horse or mouse - has never been bred, nor is it ever likely to be. The best we can hope for is an accurate guide to what a really good animal would be, describing as clearly as possible all the relevant characteristics, and their relative importance.

The Rex standards have gradually evolved and been modified over the years. Compared to those for some breeds, they are a model of clarity, but still need a certain amount of qualification and explanation, if the novice is to get a true understanding of what is required. With the odd exception, which will be dealt with when appropriate, the requirements for coat and type are the same for all Rexes, and are allocated forty and twenty points respectively. Colour is treated in individual chapters and carries forty points.

The British Rabbit Council has published a Breed Standards Book in colour, with loose leaf pages in a specially designed binder so that new standards can be added from time to time. Full colour photographs of most of the varieties described in this book are included.

The Breed Standards Book is available to all fanciers. The address of the British Rabbit Council is listed on page 211.

The author judging Chinchilla Rex at Bradford Championship Show

COAT

Obviously the most striking attribute of the Rex, and at one time carried fifty points. It is perhaps debatable whether putting colour and coat on an equal footing has really benefited the breed, but this is hardly the place to re-open that discussion. Suffice it to say that, however good its colour, a poor coated Rex will get nowhere in competition; in fact, many coat failings will also affect the colour to some extent, so how do we define a good rex coat? The standard does it in the following terms:

"To be approximately half an inch in length. Fine, silky texture free from harshness and woolliness, intensely dense, smooth and level over the whole body, of a lustrous sheen, firm and plush-like character, devoid of projecting guard hairs".

A very comprehensive description of what some might call the blindingly obvious, but the novice might find a little difficulty in reconciling some apparent contradictions. How, for example, can the coat be silky and yet firm? Given all the other parameters, it can, but a slight failing in one direction may well affect everything else.

Probably the most important single aspect is the length of the coat. Whilst we do not need the half-inch to micrometer accuracy, the closer we can get to it, the better. In theory, the coat could grow to less than half an inch; what effect this would have on the texture is really a matter of conjecture, as the opposite tendency is the most usual condition.

Slightly excessive length is no detriment - we are, after all, only looking for an approximate figure. Anything much more than an eighth of an inch over, and we begin to find trouble. There will be an entirely false sense of added density; instead of standing more or less vertically, the fur will tend to lie flat, and there is no chance of achieving a plush-like feel. Although the coat may well be silky, it cannot have that firm 'body' when stroked from tail to nape unless it is as close to the standard length as possible.

Guard hairs projecting above the surface are obviously to be avoided. Sometimes they are scattered at fairly wide intervals over the body, and are very often of little greater diameter than the hairs of the undercoat. To this extent they are more of a visual fault, as they can rarely be felt when assessing the texture. Fortunately, they can usually be groomed out: a nylon stocking over the hands is very effective for this. Blues and Lilacs seem to be particularly prone to this type of guard hair, and as they are usually very dark in colour, they will be immediately apparent to the judge. One has to wonder why they were not so apparent to the exhibitor, who could easily have groomed them out!

The other type of projecting guard hair cannot be so easily treated. These project only slightly above the undercoat, but are so profuse that they sometimes give the appearance of ticking. They are decidedly coarser than the rest of the fur, and completely ruin both the texture and levelness of the coat. Perversely, a rabbit with a coat like this is only a little short of perfection! If the guard hairs were only a little shorter – down to the level of the underfur – the coat would look perfectly level, and have a very pronounced plush texture.

There is, then, a very fine dividing line between success and failure as far as levelness and texture are concerned. Contrary to first impressions, the rex coat is not devoid of guard hairs. If it were, it would be lacking in density, excessively fine in texture, and by no stretch of the imagination would it resemble plush. If we were still aiming at the fur trade, they would rightly reject such a pelt as lacking in hard-wearing properties. The guard hairs must be there, slightly thicker in diameter than the undercoat hairs, but of the same length. They must be sufficient in number to give the necessary resilience to the coat, but not so numerous as to impart a harshness.

This aspect is very much bound up with density, which is simply the number of hairs to the square inch. If the proportion of guard hairs is too high, in a very dense coat there will be little or no movement to the fur when it is stroked or blown into. This is a condition very often found in bucks; they grow such a thick coat that they never seem to moult clear, and very often suffer from scurf, presumably because not enough air can get to the skin. Obviously, they have no future on the show bench, but are invaluable for breeding, as a balance to the type of doe which is slightly too silky.

Some would go as far as to say that a buck with a good show coat should never be bred from, and that many of the faults in today's stock stem from breeding from too finely-textured animals. I am inclined to agree with this view; if it were possible to conduct a long term analysis it would probably be found that the majority of excellent show animals were bred from parents which themselves never quite made the grade.

The other problem which can stem from a lack of guard hairs is woolliness, where the hairs tend to stick to their neighbours. The dilute colours such as the Blues and Lilacs again seem to suffer more from this problem than the other breeds, and it is usually associated with a pronounced curl in the belly and groin fur which never clears.

Any trace of woolliness will, of course, detract from the final attribute we require, the lustrous sheen. This does not mean that we want our Rexes to look like Satins; these words were in our standard long before Satins came upon the scene. To get the level, dense coat, we have to breed for it; to apply the finishing touch of a sheen, we need to feed for it. We want the gloss to the coat which can only come from perfect health and grooming. Never be tempted to apply this sheen by artificial means; it will come from oils produced within the rabbit, not wiped on from the outside.

To consistently breed good coats, then, we must make sure to breed only from stock which is near enough to the half-inch mark, and balance the coarser textures with the finer ones. This is a simple matter of applied genetics; it will be found that density is not entirely hereditary, and may well be enhanced by good environmental conditions, as will the sheen.

Three Bradford rex champions excelling in type. Top M E Bevan's Chinrex;
centre Harrison & Carpenter's Ermine; bottom J J Webb's Lynx

TYPE

"Well proportioned and graceful carriage, the body sloping gently up to well-rounded quarters set on strong hind legs, medium bone. Head bold and broad, ears erect and to be in proportion to body; dewlap should not be excessive, eyes and toe-nails should preferably match the body colour.
WEIGHT. For adults 6 to 8 lbs."

This is probably the least self-explanatory section of the standard, and the one most open to different interpretations. It is obviously difficult, if not impossible, to adequately describe a living, three-dimensional shape in words. Nevertheless, whilst most experienced breeders and judges would probably find it easier to describe bad type, they might agree with me that good type starts at the shoulders.

Viewed from the side, the shoulders should be sufficiently deep and strong as to hold the rabbit's chest clear of the ground. They need to be well tucked in to the rib cage, with sufficient width to be easily seen behind the head when viewed from the front. The front legs must be fairly short - extending just an inch or so in front of the head when the animal is relaxed. Medium bone is called for, too heavy will give the appearance of coarseness, whilst if it is too fine it will lack the strength to support the weight of the head and shoulders, and may also contribute to loss of fur on the pads.

The head itself needs to be set on a fairly short neck, and held well up. Whilst we do not want anything like the proportions of the New Zealand White – or even the Dwarf – it needs to be thoroughly in proportion to the rest of the body. Whilst a buck will obviously have the broader and more rounded skull, even a doe should show no angularity or 'snipiness'.

Whilst every adult doe will have a dewlap of some sort, it must be as small as possible consistent with its purpose. That is, to act as a reserve store of fat, and a doe without a dewlap at all cannot possibly be fit. Nevertheless, an excessive dewlap is held to be a disqualification, although regrettably the standard gives us no guidance as to what is to be regarded as excessive. This is very much a matter for the discretion of each individual judge, hardly ideal for a disqualifying fault! In practice, a doe with nice broad shoulders and good head carriage will be able to support quite a large dewlap without it appearing obtrusive, whereas one with narrow shoulders and head can scarcely carry a dewlap at all which does not look ugly. In some does, the dewlap covers almost the entire chest, and the front feet when she lies down. To my mind, this is definitely excessive, although its owner might not agree!

The ears need to be of good substance and covered with fur. The thin, 'papery' type are almost invariably very sparsely furred, and spoil the appearance of far too many rabbits. In length, they should just reach the end of the shoulder blades when held flat; the novice should note that, in young stock, the ears are invariably longer, this being Nature's way of dissipating excess heat. Provided that they are bred from parents with ears of the correct length, the youngsters will invariably 'grow into' their ears as they mature.

From the nape, the spine needs to rise at a gentle slope towards the hindquarters, and then curve in an arc to the tail. It is most important that it does this at a constant radius, so that there is no trace of squareness to the rump.

A big problem in the early days was the "chopped-off" rump. This was, in fact, an inherited deformity of the spine which has virtually been bred out; the backbone, instead of curving, bent at a very sharp angle; this also distorted the pelvic joint, making the hind legs jut out almost at right angles. It was a most unsightly effect, and could not have improved the general well-being of the rabbit. No animal which exhibits such a tendency should be retained.

The condition should not be confused with the "square" rump, which is much more often seen. Here, the backbone comes down in a straight line rather than a curve, and also allows the "pin-bones" in the pelvis to be too prominent. It may well be that this is just a less-pronounced deformity than the "chopped-off" rump, but it is not, and never has been, grounds for disqualification as some would have us believe. Nevertheless, it is an ugly fault, and very easy to breed into a strain.

The hind legs themselves need to be strong without coarseness, of moderate length and carried perfectly straight fore and aft, well tucked in to the sides. A common fault is for them to splay outwards, which spoils the carriage. In all probability this is an inbred deformity, to be avoided in breeding stock at all costs.

How long should the body be? How long is a piece of string? As with all other aspects of the Rex type, moderation is the key word. Too little length results in cobbiness, which is not wanted. Too much will produce snakiness, which is probably an even worse fault from a commercial point of view. If when the rabbit is lying on a flat surface, the hindquarters nearly touch the forelegs, this would be cobbiness, and we would not get a gentle slope of the backbone. Too big a gap and the animal is too long in the barrel. Probably a gap of one and a half to two inches is about right, although much will depend on the overall size of the rabbit.

With a weight tolerance between six and eight pounds, obviously there can be a considerable difference in size between two animals which, on paper, are of equal merit. However, if a fully mature exhibit is to fulfil all the other parameters of type and coat, most breeders would hold that the weight should be much nearer the top limit than the bottom. We should bear in mind that a Rex is technically an adult at five months of age, but will not reach full maturity until at least eight weeks after that. Therefore, to be fair, the lower limit must be set to accommodate this age group, in the almost certain knowledge that their ultimate weight will be higher.

I would always take a very jaundiced view of a fully mature Rex which struggles to make the bottom weight limit. It may have suffered from stunted growth, in which case its head and limbs will probably be out of proportion to the rest of the body. If everything is in balance, the bone will be fine rather than medium.

At the other end of the scale, anything much over eight pounds is likely to be the result of excess fat and/or coarseness of bone, both of which will detract from the type. Nevertheless, half a pound overweight is an error of six and a quarter percent, whilst half a pound underweight is more than eight percent off the target, and is clearly the greater fault.

Quite definitely, though, the smaller exhibits must be avoided for their probable effect on future generations. For a variety of reasons, with any form of selective breeding the easiest characteristic to lose is size. Whilst two six pound Rexes may just fit the standard, it is a very safe bet that their progeny will not. Whilst underweight is not a disqualification from the judging table, the wise fancier will treat it as such from the breeding pen.

This Sable buck bred by Alwyn Scott excels type

Finally, we must note that the weights quoted are for adult rabbits, and divergences are faults rather than disqualifications. There are no limits stipulated for young stock, and the practise of some judges disqualifying under five months exhibits purely because they weigh six pounds must be severely called into question. There can be nothing more heart-breaking than to nurture a youngster - possibly the sole survivor of a litter, to show it with its teeth, joints and finish clearly showing that it is still under five months and then get it thrown off the table just because it comes within the adult weight limit. Of course it will; an eight pound adult is perfectly permissible, and will almost certainly have weighed well over six pounds at five months. There is NO disqualification on weight grounds for any Rex, young or adult, other than the Mini-rex.

Although only twenty points are allotted to type, in practise it is much easier to lose half the allocation than it would be to drop ten points on coat or colour. A slight failing in, say, body or ear length may be no major detriment in exhibition, and can usually be corrected by a suitable partner in the breeding pen. Most of the other faults – particularly lack of size – are much more difficult to eliminate.

For the novice breeder seeking his foundation stock, my advice would be to ignore the points allotment and put good type as the number one priority. If you start off with good type and size, it is no great problem to keep it, and you can thus concentrate on colour and coat in the breeding plans. Badly shaped stock, of small size, will never breed winners, which is what the game is all about.

FAULTS AND DISQUALIFICATIONS

Strictly speaking, a divergence from the written standard in any respect must lose points, and is thus a fault. In the course of time it has been found that certain problems are so serious that they require more specific instructions to the judge, and they have to be listed separately, so that no-one is given any excuse for overlooking them!

Some faults are applicable only to certain varieties or colours, and these are dealt with within the individual standards. Others can, and do, affect all varieties, and are listed separately. Whilst the distinction between a fault and a disqualification is obvious, it is perhaps regrettable that the standard makes no attempt to grade the faults in order of seriousness: thus, if one exhibit has bare pads, and its nearest competitor has white hairs, the standard gives no guidance as to which is to be considered the worst fault. One judge might say that bare pads can easily lead to sore ones, and are therefore next door to a disqualification. Another might just as easily say that they are curable, whereas white hairs can never improve without cheating, and may well be more of a hereditary problem. It is these slight divergences of opinion which adds to the interest – and frustration – of exhibiting. Most of the faults are self-explanatory, but I will list them all, with comments where appropriate.

NARROW WEDGE HEAD.

DROOPING EARS.

No problem in recognising this condition: the only difficulty is in trying to decide how serious it is. The judge must obviously fault it, but the owner has rather more of a problem. If the rabbit was perfectly alright when he brought it to the show then it may well be entirely due to the heat of the venue, particularly if it is a tent in midsummer. If he knew the rabbit had a tendency to drop his ears, then perhaps it should not have been shown; more importantly, in the long term, is it wise to continue showing and, maybe, breeding from the animal?

If a youngster, with no trace of the fault in its parentage, the condition may well improve with age and the animal will be able to be shown. On the other hand, lopped ears are hereditary, and it could easily be the case that both parents carried the faulty gene without showing its effects themselves. One would need to be very careful indeed to breed from this sort of animal, and be prepared to have to cull it, its progeny and its parents, should the fault persist into future generations.

BARE PADS

In this condition, both the front and back feet may be devoid of hair - even slightly inflamed. The cause and treatment have been dealt with elsewhere. On most Rex, the skin at the "elbow" joint of the back feet can usually be seen, as can the toes of the front feet. This will not normally be unduly penalised in the Rex classes, but other judges will undoubtedly make hay in the duplicates!

Once the skin has been broken, there is absolutely no point in showing the rabbit until the condition has been treated.

THIN OR CURLY TRIANGLE

This is the area just behind the ears, otherwise known as the nape. In the past, some rabbits never managed to grow much hair in this region, and if we happen to breed one which is consistently short of fur here, it should be disposed of. More often, though, the condition is caused by moult, the nape almost always being the last place to finish.

WHITE HAIRS ON COLOURED COATS

The standard goes on to say that this must not be confused with ticking on ticked varieties. This does not mean that Martens and Foxes do not suffer from white hairs - they do, and both judge and breeder must be clear on the distinction between ticking and white hairs.

Ticking is a white tip to a coloured hair, whereas a white hair will be white right down to the undercolour. From an exhibition point of view, it does not much matter whether the white hairs consist of a few prominent guard hairs which are immediately obvious, or a profusion in the undercoat which can only be seen when the judge blows into the fur: in either case, the rabbit is going to be faulted.

LACK OF DENSITY, HARSH, WAVY, WOOLLY OR CURLY COATS

Not much else to be said, apart from the obvious fact that a waved coat is permissible in Satinrex – and obligatory in the Astrex!

ADULTS OVER OR UNDERWEIGHT
See comments in the chapter on type.

BLACK HAIRS IN BLUES AND LILACS
Quite a common fault, usually seen as fairly widely spaced guard hairs. A fairly heavy grooming should usually remove them, but selective breeding is the long-term solution.

DISQUALIFICATIONS

ILL-HEALTH
Perfectly obvious in most cases, except possibly when the rabbit gives just one sneeze on the judging table. Some judges will automatically disqualify, others may attribute it to something temporary like dust, nerves or the bright light. In such a case, provided the insides of the front legs are not matted – which would indicate a long-term problem – a judge might take a chance and allow the rabbits to stay on the table. From a purely personal viewpoint, I think that is too big a chance to take if there is the slightest trace of mucus present. Major epidemics have been started from lesser causes.

PUTTY NOSES
A white nose or one devoid of fur. Most Foxes and Martens will carry a small spot on the end of the nose, usually with a few more white hairs around it; whilst this is disfiguring, it does not rank as the true putty nose, which will practically cover the organ.

WHITE PATCHES
Caused by a simple recessive gene, and disfigured some of the early Mini-rex. They can be hidden by the white patterning in Agouti and Tan-patterned rabbits, and then passed on to their self-coloured progeny. Although they can appear on any part of the body, under the chin and the end of the front feet seem to be their favoured locations.

They can also be caused by damage to the skin, either during birth or in later life. These will not be hereditary, although one would need to be absolutely certain of the cause before freely breeding from an affected animal.

A disqualification, whatever the cause. As a matter of interest, they can easily result from the burn caused by cigarette ash, which is one of the reasons why smoking is no longer allowed at the judging table.

CROOKED LEGS

Generally caused by rickets, with a hereditary condition added to dietary deficiencies. As such it is not a condition we often see today; in fact, whenever I have seen crooked legs, they were caused by completely the opposite to a dietary deficiency. Twice I have had a litter with a single youngster, which grew so quickly that I believe they literally grew to fit the shape of the nest, and finished up with front legs considerably bowed. Acting on Mark Twain's definition of experience being "recognising a mistake the second time you make it", I now make it a rule to enlarge the nest slightly every day, so the youngster has got room to move.

EXCESSIVE DEWLAP

Very difficult to define precisely, see the chapter on Type.

SORE PADS

Where the skin is broken or scabbed. Cause and treatment already dealt with.

SPECKLED, WALL OR ODD COLOURED EYES

Not very often seen - I often wonder if we look hard enough! A wall eye is a very pale blue, not to be confused with the grey colour sometimes found in Chinrex. In this breed, the eyes can be either brown or grey - but not both!

GENETICS AND THE REX

Mention the word genetics to the average rabbit fancier, and he'll run a mile. Whilst it must be admitted that, if one is only interested in breeding one colour of one breed, it can be done with no knowledge of genetics, it is nevertheless true that any successful breeding system will be based on sound genetic principles, even though the fancier may be unaware of the fact.

Furthermore, it would be a very rare stud which did not produce the odd animal which was not the same colour as its parents, even after many generations of line breeding. If this should happen in the first litter a novice bred from expensive foundation stock, he might well consider himself the victim of a confidence trick; a little knowledge of very elementary genetics would soon dispel this notion.

It is often said that the only genetic rule worth knowing is that "like breeds like". The more one considers this age-old saw, the less true it appears! It might be more realistic to say that like rarely breeds like when you want it to, but always does when you don't! Thus, two animals showing the same fault will almost always produce offspring which are similarly faulty; the two perfect specimens which, by their appearance, should breed a litter of champions, will often produce nothing but rubbish. The founding fathers of our fancy were, of course, aware of these phenomena, long before the laws of genetics were investigated and published; in fact, many genetic discoveries have been based on work carried out on rabbits, particularly the Rex.

Whilst - with one possible exception - it is unlikely that a Rex fancier is going to produce something previously unknown to science, it will be obvious from later sections of this book that certain varieties, once popular, are hovering on the verge of extinction, if they haven't already reached it.

It is for this reason that I felt it better to put this chapter ahead of those on individual breeds. The recovery of the rarer ones would be, in most cases, quite feasible, capable of being undertaken by anyone with the time, space and a little knowledge. It is the aim of this chapter to supply that knowledge, without delving at all deeply into the realms of molecular biology. Whilst the 'A' level student may be quite happy to bandy such words as 'chromosome', 'heterozygote' and 'deoxyribonucleic acid' with all and sundry, your average rabbit fancier would not, and with good reason. All he is interested in, in terms of experimental breeding, is what happens if A is crossed with B - in the words of W.S. Gilbert, "Never mind the why and wherefore". To reach the position of being able to do this, the only necessary concept to grasp is that of the gene - not so much what a gene is, but what are its effects, and how they can be predicted, if not controlled.

The word gene itself is of comparatively recent origin, although the existence of such a body was appreciated as far back as the time of CHARLES DARWIN. Up to his time, it had been generally believed that all animals on earth were exactly the same as they were on the day their forebears were created. Darwin proved otherwise: all living things produce slight variations in their offspring. If the variation - which could be in size, colour, behaviour or any number of characteristics - gives the animal an advantage in survival over its peers, then it will tend to reproduce more successfully, and in time the variation will become fixed in the population. If the variation puts the animal at a disadvantage - e.g. a black Polar Bear - its chances of survival to reproduction are reduced. As fanciers, of course, we take advantage of these variations. By removing the environmental restraints, we are able to cultivate the abnormal individuals which would otherwise lose out in the race for survival; one of the most striking examples of this we have, of course, in the Rex.

Whilst Darwin realised that these variations must be initiated within the reproductive system of the animal, his researches did nothing to prove it. This was left to the proverbial 'old monk', GREGOR MENDEL, whose researches into the hereditary behaviour of the common pea can be truly said to be the basis of genetic study. Even then, he did not use the word gene, merely describing the hereditary mechanisms as 'factors' which were passed on through successive generations. What he did prove was that these 'factors' are contributed equally by the male and female plant or animal to the next generation. For every characteristic which is controlled by heredity, an animal must contain two 'factors' which work in pairs. The reproductive system must contain some mechanism whereby this pairing is broken, so that each sperm or egg only contains one of each pair, to be united with its opposite number when an egg is fertilised by a sperm to start the next generation. Mendel's knowledge of cell structure was rather limited, of course, but he knew that this division must be a basic concept - it would be physically impossible for all the factors to be passed on ad infinitum. Thus, any animal must receive half its genetic material from its father, half from its mother; equally, it receives one quarter from each of its grandparents, and so on back through the generations.

We now know how this division takes place, we have an increasing knowledge of the structure of the 'factors' which we now call genes, even though they are so small that even the most advanced microscopes can only 'see' the very biggest ones. We are able to modify the structure of some genes to produce an entirely different organism: most insulin used in the treatment of diabetes is now produced by the genetic engineering of a bacterium found in pigs' intestines. In fact, we know so much that it would be possible to produce a very thick volume of genetic facts which had some bearing on Rex rabbits - but who would want to read it?

Since we all know that it takes a successful mating between a buck and doe to produce a litter, it is not too large a step from there to accept that this litter will carry genetic material derived, in equal parts, from both parents. That is really all the knowledge Mendel had, and all we need to be able to understand the significance of his experiments. In fact, we would do well to forget about the results he obtained with the peas, and imagine what he would have done had he had some rabbits to work with; the basic principles he established would have been exactly the same.

Imagine, then, that Mendel was alive at the time the first Rex appeared, and already had a stud of normal coated rabbits. Having obtained some of the new Rexes, he would first have tried to find out whether they bred true; he would have found that they did. Likewise, whatever other variations might have occurred in the litters, all the progeny of his normal-coated stock had normal coats themselves.

His next step would have been to cross some of his Rexes with normal-coated stock. No matter whether he used a Rex buck on a normal doe, or vice-versa, he would have found exactly the same results - all the progeny would have had normal coats. The Rex coat would appear to have been lost almost as soon as it had been found. He would not, however, have thrown up his hands in despair, but would have mated this generation together. This time, whilst most of the progeny would have had normal coats, some of them would have been Rexes. Having bred a sufficient number of litters to get a meaningful quantity of young, he would have found that one quarter of the progeny had Rex coats, whilst the other three-quarters were normal.

Continuing from there, the Rexes would have been mated together, as would their normal-coated brethren. As with his original stock, all the progeny of two Rexes would have rex coats. Some of the normal coated progeny would have produced only normals when bred together, but the majority would produce some rexes, again in the proportion of one Rex to three Normals.

Taking stock of the situation, he would have realised a number of significant facts. Firstly, that the gene which controls coat length had, for some reason, changed or 'mutated' to give rise to the Rex. This mutation would not be apparent if it were inherited along with a 'normal' gene, although it could be passed on to subsequent generations.

This was proof - if proof were needed - that each parent contributes equally to the genetic make-up of their progeny. Whether it was a Rex buck or doe used in the original cross made no difference - the progeny were all normal-coated. The fact that rex coats re-appeared in the next generation proved that the gene from the Rex grandparent had been transmitted. Without doubt, two genes were present in each animal, one inherited from each parent. In turn, the animal would pass on just one of these genes to its progeny, although the absolute proof of this depended to come extent on the explanation of the apparent disappearance of the rex coat in the first cross.

This led Mendel to formulate his theory of 'Dominance'. Although he knew that each animal contained one gene for 'Rex' and one for 'Normal', all of them appeared to have normal coats. The gene for normal coat was, if you like to think of it in those terms, 'stronger' than that for rex. A rabbit would appear to be normal coated whether it carried one 'Normal' gene or two, whereas the coat would only be rex if TWO 'Rex' genes were carried. Therefore, the 'Normal' gene was DOMINANT to the 'Rex', in that it only had to be present once to show its effects. In contrast, the 'Rex' gene was RECESSIVE and had to be present as a pair before it could become apparent. This is one of the fundamental concepts in genetic science: all genes are able to change or MUTATE, to give rise to two or more alternative forms; when this happens, one form is almost always partially or totally dominant to the other.

Mendel developed a useful form of short-hand notation which makes this type of inheritance simpler to follow. Whenever a recessive gene was identified, it was given a letter relating in some way to the effect it produced - thus for rex the letter 'r' would be allocated. A small or lower-case 'r', to indicate that it is a recessive, whilst the normal, dominant gene is given the symbol 'R'. Since we have by now, I hope, accepted that every animal must carry its genes in pairs, a pure breeding normal coated rabbit would be given the symbol 'RR', whilst a Rex would have 'rr'; as these are recessive genes, the animal is, by definition, pure-breeding. A first-generation cross between the two types will give rise to progeny with the classification 'Rr'. Note that this MUST be so. It can receive one gene only from each parent - 'R' from the normal coated parent, 'r' from the Rex. Because 'R' is DOMINANT to 'r', an 'Rr' animal will appear to have a normal coat. Look, though, what happens in the next generation: each parent can contribute either R or r to each of its offspring. The possible combinations are R from the father, R from the mother; R from the father, r from the mother; r from the father, R from the mother; or r from the father and r from the mother. Thus we get

    1: RR
    2: Rr
    3: rR
    4: rr

Types 2 and 3 are, of course, identical; they each contain one R and one r, and would normally be written Rr. Thus, in this second generation, we obtain one RR pairing, two Rr and one rr. Like their grand-parents, the RR and rr animals will breed true, whilst the Rr ones will follow the same pattern as the parents.

This can also be shown in what is known as a Punnet square, Fig. 1.

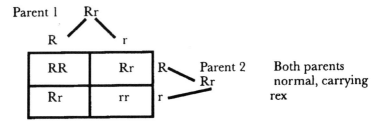

which becomes even more useful when dealing with larger combinations of genes.

This illustrates a universal principle. When each parent carries one dominant and one recessive gene, the offspring visually divide into the ratio three of the dominant type to one of the recessive.

We must, at this stage, digress a little, lest it should be thought that these proportions can be universally applied. We must not expect that every litter of four from an Rr x Rr mating will contain no more and no less than one Rex. Mendel realised this, and had to breed thousands of peas in his second generations to prove his formula. No pair of rabbits could be bred from long enough to get enough offspring to conform exactly to the theoretical numbers, other than by chance - it is, in fact, chance that determines the gene pairings in the first place.

Consider the male rabbit, carrying the Rr combination. It is at the stage when he produces sperm that the gene pairing is split, so that half his sperm will carry 'R' and the other half 'r'. Since he produces probably a million million sperm at a time, it is a very reasonable proposition that each mating will result in 50% 'R' sperm and 50% 'r'. The doe's eggs are a rather different proposition. Before she was even born she would have developed something like a million eggs in her ovaries - half with the 'R' gene and half with 'r'. Nothing like the quantity of sperm which the male could produce, of course, but still sufficient to be able to say that if all these eggs could be fertilised at once the offspring would be 25% RR, 50%Rr and 25% rr exactly.

Of course, this does not happen. Some of the eggs may die in the ovaries; probably not more than twenty may be shed at each ovulation, of which half or more will fail to be fertilised, or die as embryos; she may undergo a false pregnancy, in which case, however many eggs she produces, none will be fertilised. Equally, she may well die without ever shedding more than a very small proportion of her eggs. All in all, the chances of her producing live offspring in the exact proportions predicted are remote in the extreme, but nevertheless the formula still holds good.

Imagine you are tossing a coin. It must land heads or tails, and in the long run it will do so in equal proportions; yet one can never predict how it will land on any one toss - especially if you're the England cricket captain! Just so with the rabbits; if you are expecting one rex in four, and get none in a litter of eight does not disprove the theory - you might get six next time round. All that can be said is that, the more offspring are bred, the closer the proportions will approximate to the theoretical ones.

To return to our original example, the method of inheritance of the rex coat. Suppose we had just the one Rex buck, and wanted to produce as many rex as possible before he turned up his heels. We know that his offspring via a cross to the normal will all be normal coated, but produce 25% rex in the second generation, if we can breed sufficient youngsters in total to give the formula a chance to work. Is there a better way? Look what would happen if we took a first-cross doe (Rr) and mated her back to her (rr) father.

Fig. 2.

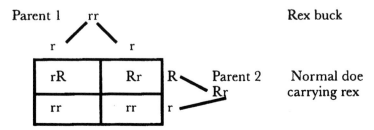

Progeny 50% Rr, 50% rr.

(Note that exactly the same result would be obtained by mating a pure Rex doe to a normal buck, carrying Rex.)

Now the proportion of rexes has doubled - in the long term it can be neither more nor less than 50%. As a matter of principle, then, whatever recessive gene we are trying to establish in our stock, we will achieve it more quickly by mating back the first generation to the parent which carries two of the genes. We can also reproduce the recessives by mating together the young from the first cross, but only in half the quantity. It may be, of course, that the Rex buck had characteristics which we did NOT want to perpetuate. If they were not evident in the first generation cross, we could be justified in assuming that they, too, were caused by a recessive gene, and we would NOT mate back to the father, since this would establish the genes in half his offspring.

This is such an important principle that it is worth leaving Mendel to consider his next step, whilst we digest some of the implications of his first discoveries.

As fanciers, we have decided that some characteristics of our animals are good, and must be perpetuated, whilst others are faults - unwanted characteristics which we would like to "breed out". If the fault is caused by a single gene, we can see even now what our plan of action must be - decide whether it is a dominant or recessive gene, and act accordingly.

Purely as an illustration, we will consider our first generation cross - Rr. As a Rex, it would carry an obvious fault - the one R gene masks the rex coat and it would not be a rex at all! However, the principle is there. If one of the parents did not carry the fault (in this case the 'rr' Rex parent), mating back to that parent would remove the faulty gene from half the offspring. Since it is a 'dominant' gene, the offspring which do not *show* its effects cannot possibly *carry* it either. If we breed only from these offspring, the fault can never re-appear.

Naturally enough, dominant genes rarely, if ever, give rise to what we call faults. They are so easily removed from the population that, to all intents and purposes they do not exist, and would not warrant a mention in the standards. Not so, however, any fault caused by a recessive gene or genes. Going back to our 'Rr' generation, imagine that now a rex coat is a fault. Although we cannot see it, all the animals carry the rex gene, and in the next generation twentyfive percent of our stock will be faulty. These can be immediately discarded, but have we "bred out" the fault? No, because whilst another twentyfive percent will be of the 'RR' type - neither displaying nor carrying the fault - the remainder of the youngsters will follow the pattern of their parents. They may **look** just like the 'RR' type, but as they carry the faulty 'r' gene they will pass it on to the next generation. Visually, we cannot separate the 'RR' sheep from the 'Rr' goats, but is there any other way of doing so?

We could carry out what we call a *'test mating'*. 'Rr' mated to 'rr', as we have seen, will produce 50% 'rr' in the litters, so even the appearance of one 'rr' will prove that the parent we are testing carries the faulty gene. What if we take a couple of test litters from a doe, and the faulty gene does NOT show up - can we assume that she is clear? Not really: although, if she carries the gene, half her offspring from a test mating should show it, we have seen that the laws of chance dictate that large numbers need to be bred. We could probably use up the entire reproductive life of a doe without being entirely certain that she did NOT carry the gene, but could prove that she DID in her very first litter. Hence, it is hardly worth carrying out test matings on a doe; much more worthwhile on a buck. If you have a sufficient number of recessive-type does to mate him with, the answer should come after just one round of litters.

If we are certain - beyond all reasonable doubt, as they say - that we have found a buck which does not carry the fault, are we out of the wood yet?

Again, not really. Admittedly, mated to an 'RR' doe he can never produce anything but 'RR', and the job is done; without another mutation, that fault can never come back. As we have seen, though, we can never be absolutely certain of proving the 'RR' combination as a doe. If, in fact, she is 'Rr', her offspring from our 'RR' buck will be 50% 'RR' and 50% 'Rr'. On the surface, the fault has gone, but it is still being carried. By religiously test mating all our bucks we could ensure that we never bred a rabbit which SHOWED the fault, and by a mathematical progression would reduce the incidence of the gene in the population, but we could never be 100% certain that we did not have just one rabbit in our stud which carried the faulty gene. Mate this rabbit to someone else's buck and you will throw away the results of twenty generations of line-breeding!

INHERITANCE OF TWO MUTATIONS

Meanwhile - back at the ranch - Mendel is considering what he should investigate next. Let's transport him forward in his time machine another fifty years or so, to when the Satin mutation appeared. This is another change, or mutation, to the gene or genes which control the appearance of the coat. With the rex, it became shorter, whilst the satin gene causes an alteration to the structure of the hairs, changing the way they reflect light. Two things needed to be considered. Firstly, was this a simple mutation to a recessive type, and, if so, was it a mutation of the same gene which gave rise to the rex coat, or was it a different gene entirely?

The first question was simply answered. Satin mated to satin bred nothing but satins. The control stock of normally coated rabbits had never bred satins. Normal coats crossed with a satin produced all normals in the first generation, but this generation mated together produced one satin out of every four youngsters. These satins bred true, as did some of the normals, but two-thirds of the apparent normals bred some satins when mated together. In other words, this was a recessive mutation which behaved in exactly the same manner as the one which had produced the rex.

The next question was whether this was yet another mutation to the 'R' gene, or was it connected with a different gene entirely: Obviously, if it was a change to the 'R' gene, then the recessives could be either rexes or satins - but not both. If it was a mutation to another gene, then the two characteristics would be inherited independently, and the satin gene could be given a new symbol.

The cross between a (long-coated) satin and a rex gave rise to normal coated young without sheen. In the next generation a considerable number of young had to be bred, but the net result was to show that, out of every sixteen rabbits bred, nine were completely normal coated, three were long-coated satins, three were ordinary rexes and one was a rex with the satin sheen - a Satin-rex.

This justified the allocation of a separate genetic symbol for the satin. The recessive 'satin' gene has the symbol 'sa' whilst its normal counterpart is 'Sa'. The usual situation as regards dominance applies. A pure Satin must be 'sa sa' and will breed true, whilst an apparent normal can be either 'Sa Sa' or 'Sa sa'. Only in the first instance will the animals breed true; the 'Sa sa' type will always breed approximately twentyfive percent satins.

Mendel believed that all variations were caused by mutations to separate genes, so that eventually all the known recessives could be combined in the one plant or animal. So far as the peas on which he carried out his experiments were concerned, this was true. All the seven characteristics which he studied were inherited independently, and thus were controlled by single mutations to separate genes.

This is not a universal law, however. Some genes have given rise to several mutations; it should be obvious that an animal could carry the original dominant gene and any ONE of the mutations. It could also carry TWO of the mutations and express whichever was dominant, or carry two identical mutated genes and express that characteristic. What it CANNOT do, however, is carry more than two variations on that original theme. There are at least a million genes at work within each of our rabbits, although we can only easily see the effects of a very few of them. In the vast majority of cases, at least one mutation will exist, sometimes as many as six variations on the original gene. These are the ones we will concentrate on; the ones where the effects are immediately obvious, and are capable of being transmitted independently. There are others which are said to be 'linked' to another gene, so that normally the two genes are transmitted together. With the possible exception of barred feet in Agouti rabbits, these need not concern us. There are still other genes which have no basic effect in themselves, but act by varying the effects of other, major, genes. These are known as 'modifiers', and we shall learn that they play a very important role in the fancier's activities. For the moment, let us summarise, in the form of diagrams, what the study of the satin and rex genes has shown us.

All progeny have normal length coats, without satinisation i.e., both recessive genes are "hidden".

Fig. 3.

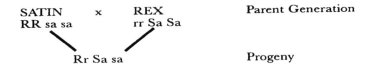

SATIN   x   REX   Parent Generation
RR sa sa   rr Sa Sa

        Rr Sa sa   Progeny

Each of the progeny in Fig. 3. can pass on the following gene combinations: R Sa, r Sa, R sa and r sa.

Fig. 4. Satin/Rex Hybrids Mated Together

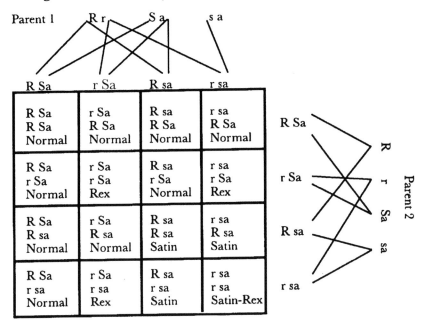

Resultant: 9 Normals, 3 Satins, 3 Rex, 1 Satin-Rex.

The 9:3:3:1 ratio holds good whenever two independent recessive genes are combined.

As we have said, there may be as many as a million genes acting in every rabbit. It would be an impossible task to identify all of them, let alone predict their inheritance. Some of them are of such major importance that their effects can easily be seen, and their inheritance predicted; the 'rex' and 'satin' genes come into this category. Others control the colour and/or pattern of the coat, and these are obviously of great interest to us; in general, they can be independently inherited, and two or more genes can act together on any particular pigment. Others are purely 'modifiers', and it might be as well to look at these now.

MODIFYING GENES

By definition, these are only identifiable by their action in conjunction with major genes. Take the 'rr' rex gene as an example. We know that some Rexes carry the dense, plush coats we are looking for; others are excessively fine and soft in texture, while yet more are long, harsh and carry a great deal of protruding guard hairs. Yet, as far as the geneticist is concerned, they are all rexes. The difference is a matter of the degree to which the rex gene is allowed to act, and this is controlled by the modifying genes, and may in many cases be traced back to the normal varieties from which the rex were derived.

Another example is the colour, brown. This can vary from the dark, "plain chocolate" shade we look for in the Havana to a much lighter, almost mealy shade. Again, to a geneticist, they are all 'Brown', and can be proved to be due to the action of a single, major gene. The variations in shade are caused by 'modifying' genes. Although, in some cases, the effects can be attributed to just two or three modifiers acting together, and behaving according to the accepted pattern of dominant/recessive, more often it is not so. Sometimes, so many genes are involved that the possible number of combinations is astronomical; in other cases, fewer genes are involved, but do not display complete dominance, so that we are looking for the effects of a particular pairing which will never breed completely true.

This is where the 'fancier' takes over from the 'geneticist'. By breeding only from those animals which seem to be approaching the ideal we have set ourselves, our stock will eventually bear little resemblance to what the geneticist gave us in the first place. Nevertheless, because we are dealing with such a great number of 'secondary' genes, which may or may not display dominance, we can never be certain of the results of any particular mating. If we could, of course, much of the fascination of the hobby would be lost!

One of the most obvious instances in which modifying genes

have been shown to be active is the Sable; this breed also shows one of the rare instances where one gene is only partially dominant to another. We shall come to that in due course, but first we must review the major genes, those which have a primary effect on the pattern or colour. About a dozen of these genes are of major interest to the rex fancier; some have mutated to give a single alternative, in' other cases there have been several. All have been given alphabetical symbols so that we can easily identify them. With one possible exception, they can all be inherited independently, so the combinations of colour and pattern we can produce, if not endless, certainly exceed those currently covered in individual standards.

The colours and patterns of the rex coat are determined by two pigments, melanin and carotene; these form clumps or granules in the hair, and it is the arrangement and concentration of these granules which determine the apparent colour of the animal. Basically, melanin pigment is black and carotene yellow, but both can be intensified or reduced by the primary genes and, possibly just as importantly, by the associated modifying genes. What we will do in this section is to define the effect of the primary genes, and then go on to analyse the known varieties of rex in terms of these genes; what the fancier must remember is that, for exhibition purposes, a certain concentration of modifying genes is also generally required if the rabbit is to meet the standard.

The basic colour, as seen in the wild rabbit, is a greyish brown, similar to the colour of the South American rodent, the Agouti. This name has been adopted by scientists to define all animals with this type of coat pattern, the dominant or 'wild' type gene being designated 'A' and, together with its mutant genes, is known as the 'Agouti' series. In some species, there are several alternatives to the basic 'A' gene, but in the rabbit there are but two.

THE AGOUTI SERIES

Gene Symbol 'A'. This gives rise to the normal wild pattern, where the two pigments can be seen separately on each hair shaft. Melanin is expressed at the base and top of the hair, whilst carotene is expressed as a band of yellow pigment towards the top of the shaft, and sometimes at the extreme tip as well, to give a form of ticking. Generally, this pattern is accompanied by a white belly and underside of the tail, together with white jowls and eye circles.

Gene Symbol 'a'ᵗ. Recessive to 'A', this gene suppresses the expression of the carotene pigment over the main body of the animal, which will thus appear a solid or 'self' colour - black in the absence of any further recessive genes. The carotene pigment is developed only in what were the white parts of the Agouti pattern, and may vary from a narrow yellowish border to a rich level tan all over the belly, etc. This is accomplished by the concentration of modifying genes.

Gene Symbol 'a'. Recessive to both 'A' and 'aᵗ', this gene completely prevents the expression of carotene. Although the pigment is still produced, its effects cannot be seen, and the animal is the same colour all over, or 'Self', the white belly and other parts also being removed by this gene.

Thus, in descending order of dominance, the Agouti series comprises:

A   Agouti pattern
aᵗ   Tan pattern
a   Self colour.

Just to reinforce what we have previously covered, every rabbit must carry two genes in each series. Due to the effects of dominance, an Agouti patterned animal could carry AA, Aaᵗ or Aa. A Tan-patterned rabbit could have aᵗaᵗ or aᵗa, whilst a Self can only carry aa. An Agouti can carry either Tan-pattern or Self as a recessive, but not both.

BLACK PIGMENTATION SERIES

Gene Symbol 'B'. This gives rise to the normal arrangement of the melanin pigment granules which appear black, or a very dark slate colour as in the Castor. In conjunction with the tan-pattern gene, it produces the Black Otter or Tan, and the Self version would be the Black.

Gene Symbol 'b'. Recessive to 'B', this gene alters the structure of the melanin pigment so that it appears brown. The Agouti version would be the Cinnamon, the Tan-pattern the Chocolate Otter and the Self the Havana.

Thus, the series comprises: B - Black
                                          b - Brown.

COLOUR SERIES

Gene Symbol 'C'. The animal has full colour.

Gene Symbol 'c^{chd}'. Dark Chinchillation. This gene eliminates the expression of carotene, so that the yellow parts of the hair become white. Thus, the Agouti version is the Chinchilla, and the Tan-pattern the Fox. The gene has no effect on a Self rabbit.

Gene Symbol 'c^{chl}'. Light Chinchillation. This gene has a similar, but more pronounced effect to the previous one. Yellow pigment is reduced to white, whilst it also has a reducing effect on black (melanin) pigment. The agouti version would be a very pale version of the Chinchilla, known as a "ghost". The Tan-pattern type is the Dark Marten Sable, and the Self a dark Siamese Sable, or Seal as the rex fancy prefers to call it.

Gene Symbol 'c^h'. Himalayan. Almost, but not quite, an Albino. Pigmentation is confined to the coolest extremities of the body, i.e. the ears, nose, tail and legs. In cold weather this may extend to include a circle around the eyes and even the dewlap. Himalayans only fit the standard if they are also genetically selfs (i.e. "aa"). Agouti patterned points can be produced, but they will be chinchillated.

Gene Symbol 'c'. Albino. If the animal possesses a pair of 'c' genes it will have no ability to develop pigment of any sort, and will be white, regardless of any other genes it may carry. These other genes will, however, be passed on, and will be expressed if the rabbit is mated to a non-albino.

Some authorities also list a medium Chinchillation gene, midway in effect between c^{chd} and c^{chl}. It is not believed that this gene exists in our stock today although some Chinchillas - normal and rex - obviously carry both c^{chd} and c^{chl}, as evidenced by the appearance of "ghosts" from time to time.

It is also very widely believed that 'c' carried as a recessive to 'c^{chl}' is responsible for the production of light and medium Sables. The same effect may be obtained by modifying genes, of which more anon. For the present, the Colour series may be said to contain, again in descending order of dominance:

C   Full Colour
c^{chd}   Dark Chinchillation
c^{chl}   Light Chinchillation

c^h Himalayan

c   Albino.

DILUTE SERIES

Gene Symbol D. Dense colour.

Gene Symbol d. Dilute. Black (melanin) pigment is diluted to a blue grey colour. There are many different shades, varying from the lavender of the Beveren to the very dark slate of the Tan. The variations are caused by concentrations of modifiers, but only in the presence of the basic genes 'dd'. In the rex, this gene gives us the Blue, the Blue Otter and, in conjunction with the Agouti gene 'A', we get the Opal.

An interesting point may have occurred to the reader. If 'bb' and 'dd' both modify the structure of the melanin pigment, what would happen if they were inherited together? Take an example: Brown (bb DD) x Blue (BB dd).

The only possible combination in the first generation is Bb Dd, thus all the young will be black, but carry the brown and dilute genes as recessives. The second generation, obtained by mating the

Parent A
BbDd

BD	Bd	bD	bd	
BD BD Black	Bd BD Black	bD BD Black	bd BD Black	BD
BD Bd Black	Bd Bd Dilute	bD Bd Black	bd Bd Dilute	Bd
BD bD Black	Bd bD Black	bD bD Brown	bd bD Brown	bD
BD bd Black	Bd bd Dilute	bD bd Brown	bd bd ?	bd bd

Parent B
BbDd

above together, is best shown by constructing a Punnet Square as we did for the Satin-rex.

The "double recessive" bb dd is well known throughout the fancy. Melanin is altered in two different ways to produce the dove-grey shade we call Lilac. With the 'A' gene we get a Lilac Agouti known as the Lynx, we can also have Lilac Otters or Tans and, of course, the Self Lilac.

The DILUTE SERIES, then, consists of:

D - Dense

d - Dilute.

EXTENSION OF YELLOW (or exclusion of Black)

Here, the 'wild' type gene, 'E' has given rise to a mutant which is dominant rather than recessive, although not completely so. There are also two further alternatives which act as normal recessives.

Gene Symbol 'E^D'. Dominant Black. This increases the development of black pigment so that, in an extreme case, an Agouti with two E^D genes would be, to all intents and purposes, a self black rabbit. It is only partially dominant to 'E', and an Agouti rex carrying one E^D and one E gene would be a dark steel. To the best of my knowledge, the E^D gene has never been introduced to the rex and will not be considered further.

Gene Symbol 'E'. Normal Yellow, as found in the Castor, Otter and Self Black.

Gene Symbol 'e^j'. Harlequin. Results in the separation of the black and yellow pigments into more or less separate bands over the body. It is of interest to note that this pattern is produced irrespective of whether the coat pattern genes are 'A', 'a^t' or 'a'.

Gene Symbol 'e'. Extension of Yellow (or exclusion of Black). The lowest recessive in this series. It results in the more or less complete removal of melanin from the coat, and an Agouti rex with two 'e' genes will have a yellow body with white belly; with suitable modifiers this will become the Orange. The tan-pattern version will - or could become - tan all over, whilst, in conjunction with the 'Self' gene, 'a', the effects of 'e' are rather less pronounced. The body colour is still yellow, but the gene fails to completely remove the black pigment from the extremities, resulting in the Tortoiseshell.

E^D	-	Dominant Black
E	-	Normal Black

eʲ   -   Harlequin

e   -   Extension of Yellow (or exclusion of Black

ENGLISH SPOTTING OR BUTTERFLY PATTERN SERIES

Opinions differ as to whether the "spotted" gene is semi-dominant or semi recessive to the normal full coloured version. Sandford has it that the gene is semi-dominant and I will follow his lead. From the fancier's point of view, there is no practical difference.

Gene Symbol 'en'. A normal colour with no spotting or pattern.

Gene Symbol 'En'. A semi-dominant mutation. If two 'En' genes are carried, the result is a white body colour with just a few coloured spots; generally, there will be a small spot on either side of the nose, a pattern known as the 'Charlie' to English fanciers because of the resemblance to the late Charlie Chaplin's moustache. It should be noted that a semi-lethal gene seems to be involved here, and the "Charlie" tends to be a weakling, and not to turn up in quite the expected proportions.

'en en' and 'En En' animals breed true; the hybrid 'En en' results in the well known Butterfly in all its ramifications. Originally, butterfly-patterned rabbits were very heavily marked, carrying some white in the shoulder region, and white on the face except around the nose, which carried the characteristic butterfly shaped pattern. This pattern still exists in various breeds of Lops, but the steady accumulation of modifying genes has resulted in the much lighter patterns shown by the English, Rhinelander and Dalmatian, together with the recently recognised Broken. The important point to note is that these will not breed true: they carry En and en genes. Mated together, this will produce En En, En en, and en en in the by now familiar proportions of 1:2:1, so that only half the offspring will be of the required pattern. Obviously, an En En Charlie mated an 'en en' Self will produce all spotted young; whether the spots will be where the fanciers wants them to be is a different matter! The series - if such it can be called, therefore consists of:

En En   -   'Charlie'

En en   -   English or Butterfly pattern

en en   -   Self

COAT LENGTH SERIES

Gene Symbol 'R'. Normal coat with protruding guard hairs.

Gene Symbol 'r'. Rex coat. Guard hairs reduced to about the same length as the undercoat; may be finer in diameter, and fewer in number, although these latter aspects may well be attributable to modifiers.

The mode of inheritance of the rex coat has already been discussed in sufficient detail, but it may not be generally realised that other mutations have occurred which gave rise to the same effect. Thus, apart from the rexes bred by Gillet, there was a further mutation in Germany and one - possibly two - in the Normandy region of France. The German mutation resulted in a somewhat coarser coat than Gillet's, and is not believed to have been persevered with. The Normandy versions were indistinguishable from Gillet's; since they occurred very close to each other both in time and place, they may well have originated from the same ancestral stock, and were thus due to the same mutation. They were not, however, due to a mutation of the same gene which produced Gillet's stock, as was proved when the two strains were bred together: the result was normal-coated youngsters!

How could this come about? How could two recessives produce a dominant? It can only be because a mutation of two different genes produced the same physical effect. If we call the Gillet mutation r1 it will have the dominant counterpart R1. Thus r1 r1 will be a rex, R1 R1 or R1 r1 will have normal coats, and this will be true whatever other genes they carry. Suppose another, entirely separate gene exists: call it R2. Let it mutate to a recessive r2 which, carried in a pair (or in duplex to get slightly more technical) results in r2 r2 and is a rex-coated animal apparently identical to the Gillet version.

Gillet's animals will have the genes r1 r1 and R2 R2.

The other version (Normandy) will have genes R1 R1 and r2 r2.

Since they both carry a pair of 'rex' genes they will look like rexes and breed true until the two strains are mixed. Then we get the combinations R1 r1, R2 r2. Since every animal carries one dominant 'non-rex' gene in each pairing, they must all have normal coats. If we were to construct a Punnet square as we did for the Satin-Rex, we would find that the second generation would result in nine normal coats (eight of which would carry one or both rex genes), three Gillet type rex, three Normandy rex and one which carried both 'rex' genes.

I have very recently learned that Gillet's original pair of Rexes did not at first breed true, some normal coats still appeared until three generations had been bred. This could, of course have been because one of his original pair was not a true rex, but merely a very short-coated normal. Equally, it could be that one of them carried both the 'rex' genes, which would account for the appearance of the occasional normal. Unfortunately, as Gillet always regretted, he did not buy the parents of his rexes, and he lost the original rex doe after her second litter. By the time the geneticists got involved, the Gillet strain was pure, breeding nothing but rexes, and it is this one which was imported into this country. Nevertheless, the Normandy strain may well still exist on the Continent; any imports of this stock will produce normal coats when mated to our own rexes.

For practical purposes, however, we may consider this series as:

    R   -   Normal coat

    r   -   Rex coat

SATINISATION SERIES

This we have already covered in sufficient detail. We only have:

Gene symbol Sa - normal coat

Gene symbol sa - satinised coat

SILVERED SERIES

Gene symbol Sl - Normal colour

Gene symbol sl - Silvered.

These genes have given rise to some controversy, in that there are so many degrees of silvering. It may be relatively sparse, affecting only the tips of some guard hairs - as we see in the Silver Grey and Silver Seal - but in the Argente the undercoat is also affected so that the overall effect is much more pronounced. It has never been satisfactorily established whether this is due to a separate gene, or merely very intense concentration of modifiers. Since the Silver Seal has never made much headway, there is little point in labouring the matter further, although it should be noted that the 'sl' gene may not be completely recessive - which could account for a lot of the white hairs in coloured coats.

WIDE BAND SERIES

Gene Symbol W. Normal band of yellow on the Agouti hair shaft, relatively narrow.

Gene Symbol w. Wider band of yellow, half the length of the hair shaft or more, as found in most exhibition Agouti rexes.

We must note that, although the effects of the gene are only seen if inherited along with 'A', it is present in all rabbits, Agouti or not. If, for example, a Castor carrying 'ww' were to be mated with a Black, the latter could contribute either 'W' or 'w'. If the latter, the young would have a wide band of tan, but it is more usual for the 'W' gene to be contributed, in which case the young would have a very dark top and hardly any tan. To conform to standard, the Castor, Lynx, Opal and Cinnamon must obviously have a constitution 'ww'. This is not necessarily the case with the Chinrex, where a narrower band of near-white is allowed. Some may carry the 'W' gene, the extra width being obtained by modifiers. If these modifiers were passed on to an animal with 'ww' constitution, the result might well be a slate band which is far too narrow.

WAVED SERIES

Gene Symbol Wa. Normal coat.

Gene Symbol wa. Waved coat. This gene is - or was - responsible for the Astrex. It should be noted that it can be carried by any rabbit - rex or normal - but is only fully expressed in a rex rabbit with a very fine coat, and then only in conjunction with modifiers. Believed to be extinct, but it is always possible that it exists still, masked by normal coat genes.

There are, of course, other genes responsible for such as the Angora and Dutch. They are either irrelevant to the rex, or too complicated to have ever been evaluated, and need not concern us here.

GENETIC CONSTITUTION OF THE BREEDS OF REX

Now that we have established the effects of the major genes, we are in a position of being able to 'construct', as it were, a rex rabbit to show how the genes interact to give the varieties we know - and one or two which have not yet made an appearance in the show pen.

To simplify matters somewhat, we will ignore some of the minor genes:

E^D is not believed to exist in any of our current rex breeds.

ww will be taken as being common to all Agoutis, and irrelevant to others, although it is believed by some authorities that it may lighten the body colour of the Tortoiseshell and its cousins.

rr is common to all rex, and will be assumed to exist in all examples.

Sa and sa, the satin genes, have already been fully enough considered. It may be taken as read that, in any example we cover, the substitution of sa sa for Sa Sa will result in the satinised version.

Wa and wa, unfortunately, cannot be considered due to the apparent extinction of wa.

With the foregoing exceptions, let us consider a Rex carrying all the dominant genes. Its genetic constitution could be written as:

AA BB CC DD EE

    AA signifies Agouti.

    BB signifies black pigmentation.

    CC signifies full colour - not chinchillated.

    DD signifies dense colour - not diluted.

    EE signifies normal yellow.

The rabbit is thus a Castor and (an extreme rarity!) a true breeding one, since we have stipulated that it carries two dominant genes in each pair. In practice, of course, it could carry any number of recessive genes which would not be apparent to the eye. For example, the above rabbit could have the make-up AA, Aa^t, or Aa and still look like a Castor. The scientist adopts a form of short-hand to signify this, and would describe the animal as 'A+', the '+' being used to indicate that any of the possible alternatives might be carried. In cases where both genes must be present for their effect to be seen, of course the '+' sign could not be used. So, we would more properly describe the Castor as:

A+B+C+D+E+

Now let's see the effect of introducing the various alternatives in turn. This is going to be a very long ride!

aᵗ+B+C+D+E

The Tan-pattern gene replaces the Agouti, resulting in the Black Otter. Any Otter can become a Tan with the necessary modifying genes, so this point must be taken as read from now on.

aa B+C+D+E+

Note that the '+' symbol cannot be used here: both 'a' genes must be present to give us this rabbit, which is the self Black.

A+bb C+D+E+

This is an Agouti rabbit which is 'brown' rather than 'black', i.e. a Cinnamon.

Aᵗ+bb C+D+E+

Tan pattern here, so we have the Chocolate Otter.

aa bb C+D+E+

The 'Self' gene gives us the Havana.

A+B+cᶜʰᵈ+D+E+

An Agouti rabbit with dark chinchillation - the Chinrex.

aᵗ+B+cᶜʰᵈ+D+E+

Tan-pattern, but chinchillated. The yellow pigment is removed from the Otter to give us a Black Fox.

aa B+cᶜʰᵈ+D+E+

A Black carrying chinchillation, but the gene has no visible effect .Note that such a rabbit might not be a very good colour for a Black, but this is due solely to the absence of the correct modifiers, not the cᶜʰᵈ gene itself.

A+bb cᶜʰᵈ+D+E+

A chinchillated Cinnamon, or brown Chinchilla. Has been shown (illegally!) as a Brown Squirrel in this country, and is known on the Continent.

aᵗ+bb cᶜʰᵈ+D+E+

Chocolate Fox.

aa bb cᶜʰᵈ+D+E+

Again, cᶜʰᵈ has no effect on a Self rabbit.

A+B+ cᶜʰˡ+D+E+

As already mentioned, light chinchillation produces a 'ghost' Chinchilla.

aᵗ+B+cᶜʰˡ cᶜʰˡ D+E+

The gene now has an effect on both black and yellow pigment.

The black of the Fox is reduced to a dark sepia, resulting in the Marten Seal.

aa B+c^{chl}c^{chl}D+E+

Black is reduced to sepia, and we have the Siamese Seal.

A+bb c^{chl}+D+E+

The brown version of the 'ghost'.

a^{t}+bb c^{chl}c^{chl}D+E+

A very pale Marten Seal, neither use nor ornament!

aa bb c^{chl}c^{chl}D+E+

A brown self, pigmentation reduced. May possibly be the Nutria?

N.B.

c^{chl} is widely believed, when inherited with 'c', the albinism gene, to result in the medium shade of Sable. Although possibly modifiers have a more prominent role, it is certainly true that very many strains of Sables produce Ermines, as well as a proportion of Seals. Accepting the hypothesis that the 'c' gene is involved, the inheritance pattern would be as follows:

c^{chl} c x c^{chl} c will produce   one c^{chl} c^{chl} (Seal)

two c^{chl} c (Sable)

one cc (Albino)

Most Seal and Sable breeders make a practice of always mating the two colours together. The combinations are thus: c^{chl} c^{chl} x c^{chl} c, giving 50% c^{chl} c^{chl}, and 50% c^{chl} c. Thus, Seals and Sables will be produced in equal proportions. As I said, modifiers have been shown to play a great part; quite possibly a c^{chl} c^{chl} animal could have such a concentration of modifiers as to approach the medium shade, in which case it could be expected to breed a greater number of Sables than Seals. In my experience, and that of many other breeders, mating Sable to Sable invariably produces a number of albinos and Seals, thereby proving that the theory that the Sable has the genetic formula c^{chl} c is true in very many cases, if not all.

A+B+c^{h}+D+E+

A Himalayan with chinchillated, agouti points, not standardised. Substituting A+ with a^{t}+ would produce tan-patterned points, again not recognised. For practical purposes we can consider only:

aa B+c^{h}+DD EE - Black Himalayan.

aa bb c^{h}+D+E+ - Chocolate Himalayan.

aa B+c^h+dd E+ - Blue Himalayan.
aa bb c^h+dd E+ - Lilac Himalayan.

++ ++ cc ++ ++
Ermine.
As already noted, the albino gene suppresses all pigmentation. An Ermine can therefore carry any of the genes outside the 'Colour' series without showing their effects: they will only be brought to notice as the result of a cross.

A+B+C+ dd E+
The black pigment is diluted to blue, resulting in the Opal.

a^t+B+C+ dd E+
Blue Otter.

aa B+C+ dd E+
Self Blue.

A+bb C+ dd E+
As in our example, brown and dilute combine to Lilac, and we get Lynx.

a^t+bb C+ dd E+
Lilac Otter.

aa bb C+ dd E+
Self Lilac.

A+ B+ c^{chd}dd E+
The dilute Chin, or Squirrel.

a^t+ B+ c^{chd} dd E+
Blue Fox.

aa B+ c^{chd} dd E+
Self Blue, the chinchillation having no effect.

A+ bb c^{chd} dd E+
A chincillated Lynx, would have a silvery cream appearance.

a^t+ bb c^{chd} dd E+
Lilac Fox.

aa bb c^{chd} dd E+
Once again c^{chd} has no apparent effect, this would look like a self lilac.

A+ B+ c^{chl}+ dd E+
Ghost Squirrel.

a^t+ B+ c^{chl} c^{chl} dd E+

The dilute version of the Marten Seal. As with the Sable, the combination of c^{chl} and c lightens the colour to a medium shade, so that we would then get the Marten Smoke Pearl - **a^t+ B+c^{chl}c dd E+.**

aa B+ c^{chl} c^{chl} dd E+

aa B+ c^{chl}c dd E+

Siamese Smoke Pearl, dark version above, medium/light below. The combination of **bb, c^{chl}+ and dd** is not considered significant, although a Lilac-pointed Smoke Pearl might have its attractions. Work that one out for yourself!

A+ B+ C+ D +e^{j}e^j

at+ B+ C+ D+ e^{j}e^j

aa B+ C+ D+ e^{j}e^j

All the above would be Black Harlequins, since this gene expresses itself whichever of the 'A' series is present.

++bb C+D+e^{j}e^j

Brown Harlequin.

++B+C+dd e^{j}e^j

Blue Harlequin.

++bb C+dd e^{j}e^j

Lilac Harlequin.

In all the above examples, if C^{chd+} is substituted for C+, the yellow pigment will be changed to white, resulting in the Magpie in all four colours. Substitution with c^{chl} is not recommended!

A+B+C+D+ee

'ee' eliminates black - or extends the yellow if you prefer. This rabbit is an Orange. Note that it is an Agouti!

a^t+B+C+D+ee

The true 'Tan-patterned' Orange, which has previously been recognised as the Orange-Buff. To a greater or lesser extent, the white on the belly and other parts is replaced by tan.

aa B+C+D+ee

The action of 'ee' is incomplete on a Self rabbit, the extremities remaining dark if not completely black. The Tortoiseshell.

A+bb C+D+ee

Also an Orange, but of a brighter shade generally than B+ ee. It is possible that many, if not most exhibition Oranges have this make-up.

a^t+bb C+D+ee

A brighter version of the Orange Buff.

aa bb C+D+ee

Bronze, or brown Tortoiseshell. Have been produced as normal Rexes and Satin-rex, but due to an anomaly in the standards, only the Satin could be shown as a Bronze, the normal Rex would be the Sussex Gold Rex.

A+B+c^{chd} or c^{chl} D+ee

a^t+B+c^{chd} or c^{chl} D+ee

Since the action of both chinchillation genes is to eliminate yellow pigment, the result in all cases would be an off-white animal of no real interest.

aa B+c^{chd} D+ee

Chinchillated Tortoiseshell, or Seal-point.

aa bb c^{chd} D+ee

Brown Seal-point.

aa BB c^{chd} dd ee

Blue Seal-point.

aa bb c^{chd} dd ee

Lilac Seal-point.

No standards exist at present for any seal-point rexes. A lighter body shade might result if the c^{chl} gene were present, but this would be at the expense of the intensity of the points.

A+B+C+ dd ee

The dilute Orange - or Fawn.

a^t+B+C+ dd ee

Never standardised, this would be fawn all over.

aa B+C+ dd ee

Dilute Tortoiseshell, as in the Beige.

A+bb C+ dd ee

Fawn, possibly a better shade for showing than B+ dd ee.

a^t+bb C+ dd ee

Again, fawn all over.

aa bb C+ dd ee

Lilac Tortoiseshell, as in the Sussex Cream.

That completes our survey of the action of the major genes. It may not be apparent, but any rabbit which carried 'En en' in addition to all the others would be a Dalmatian - although very few of the possible colour combinations are actually recognised. If e^j e^j are inherited along with 'En en', the colours will separate to produce the Tricolour. The recessive e^j e^j, en en will be a Harlequin.

I hope the reader - who may well need to go over this chapter several times - will by now have a better idea how the various colours have come about, and how they are related. The practical importance, of course, lies in determining the best way to go about recreating breeds which have been lost, or to improve those where numbers are now so low that they are about to be lost.

I have, in the chapters on individual breeds, drawn the readers' attention to those in need of revival, and suggested how this might be accomplished. It might be worthwhile considering why the revival should be necessary in the first place, and in most cases this may be attributed to fanciers (unwittingly usually) following certain genetic principles whilst ignoring others which in the long term may be more important.

I hope my friends in the Lilac fraternity will forgive me for taking their breed as an example, but this is a classic case where a breed, never very strong in numbers, has now reached the position where the current breeding stock is giving rise to such small litters that the population can barely be maintained, let alone increased.

Most, if not all, the current breeders can trace their stock to a strain which was very successful in the 1970's. When this was dispersed, nearly every Lilac-rex breeder in the country got some; from the exhibition point of view, the stock was so superior that it made sense to concentrate on it, rather than the other inferior strains. The original breeder had, by rigorous selection, eliminated any dominant genes that gave rise to inferior stock. Recessives, of course, he could never completely breed out but, in general, litters in this strain were of extremely level quality, and genetic purity as high as one could possibly have expected.

All this, however, was on the surface. The genes which produced the effects required by sight and touch were certainly carried by the vast majority of the strain. Unfortunately, beneath the surface other genes were at work producing effects which, in the long term, would prove almost catastrophic.

These genes are known as 'lethals' or 'semi-lethals'. What they do is to so affect the development of the embryos that they die in the womb, or shortly after birth. Some are recessive, whilst many more are semi-dominant, very like the En gene which causes English spotting in its hybrid state (En en). As previously noted, some authorities have suggested that the En gene is itself a 'semi-lethal', in that the En En 'Charlies' tend to be weaklings; many English breeders' records have shown that fewer 'Charlies' are born than selfs, which would suggest that many embryos die before birth, since the proportions of selfs and 'Charlies' should, in the long term be equal. Certainly, in mice, some colours are 'linked' to a semi-dominant lethal gene, so that the exhibition colour or pattern is always a hybrid; the 'pure' version is never born.

Be that as it may, it is obvious that one or more lethal genes have been bred into the Lilac Rex. They cannot be dominant: if this were so, all the young which carried even one of the genes would die before birth, whilst those which were born could not possibly carry or transmit the gene. Their litters would be of normal size. The gene or genes must therefore be either partially or totally recessive. I incline to the latter view, and believe that there are at least two at work. If we look back to the Punnet square in which we saw how the Lilac itself was produced, but now imagine that 'b' and 'd' are recessive, lethal genes, we can easily see that nearly half the expected progeny will die in the womb, since they carry a pair of one or the other lethal genes. Of the rest, the vast majority will carry the genes to the next generation.

The one fundamental principle which previous breeders overlooked was not to have taken note of the small litter sizes earlier. An outcross to another, unrelated strain, would have reduced the incidence of the lethal genes. Now, of course, such a strain does not exist, and more drastic action is called for. I have outlined my thoughts on what I think this action ought to be in the chapter devoted to the Lilac. There are many other colours where a similar course needs to be followed, and I hope that this chapter will have provided a sufficient background to enable the average fancier to do this.

The underlying principle in all cases is to bring in genes which will overcome the effects of the ones we have accidentally 'established' in our strain, without bringing in others which we then have to breed out. Obviously, therefore, if there is another, unrelated strain of the colour or breed we should first try an outcross to this, since we are at least sure that the primary 'colour' genes are there.

This may not always be possible - there may not even be another breeder, yet alone another strain. Here, another colour must be introduced, but we must be sure that its genetic constitution is as close as possible to that of our own. Hence the advice regarding the Lilac: a cross to the Havana or Blue only introduces one unwanted dominant. The outcome of breeding the offspring of this first cross together will be one Lilac in every four young. Not a very high proportion, but four times higher than if we had had to cross the Blue and Havana to actually recreate the breed. Of course, if we were to backcross this first generation to the Lilac, we should get 50% of our youngsters the right colour. More stock to work with, but twice the chance that they carry the very lethal genes we are trying to eliminate. In the long run it must pay to ignore the original, faulty, stock once we have made the first cross.

STARTING FROM SCRATCH

As we have seen, there are far more colours possible in the Rex than we have standards for. In some cases, of course, we have standards but no rabbits; these breeds must be re-created, and I have given some pointers on how to do this in later chapters. There are several Normal Fur breeds which, as yet, have no rex counterparts, and it would be a useful exercise to see how these could be produced. We could do no better than look at one of the latest fur breeds to be standardised, the Sussex.

With the Rex coat and type, the Sussex Gold would be a brown Tortoiseshell, and the Cream a Lilac Tortoiseshell, i.e. aa bb C+ D+ ee, and aa bb C+ dd ee. First thoughts might be to get hold of a Sussex and cross it with a rex of some description, but this would be neither necessary nor advisable. No Normal coat even begins to approach the Rex for density, whilst the type of the Sussex is not what we would want.

Much better to look at the genetic make-up of rexes we already have, and see if we can combine two of them to produce the colour without recourse to the Normal. The obvious starting point is the Tortoiseshell itself, which only differs from the Gold in colour by virtue of carrying B+ instead of bb. There is no rex which automatically carries bb as well as ee: some Oranges may do, but they would need to be test mated to find out. To do this we would have to use the Havana, so we might just as well use that to produce the Sussex. It carries the bb genes we required, but also E+ rather than ee.

So, assuming that neither Tortoiseshell nor Havana carry any recessives, we have:

aa BB CC DD ee rr for the Tort, and

aa bb CC DD EE rr for the Havana.

They differ only in the 'B' and 'E' series, so the other genes can be ignored. The relevant pairings are 'BB ee' and 'bb EE', and by now we should be able to predict this result without drawing diagrams.

The Tort can only contribute 'B' and 'e', whilst the Havana can only contribute 'b' and 'E' genes. Thus, the first generation will be Bb, Ee, and will be black. Mated together, these will produce nine B+ E+, three bb E+, three B+ ee, and one bb ee, that is to say, nine Blacks, three Havanas, three Tortoiseshells and one Sussex, or brown Tortoiseshell.

From here, this animal could be crossed with a Lilac. This time, all the first generation would be Havanas, their progeny resulting in nine Havanas, three Lilacs, three brown Tortoiseshells and one Lilac Tortoiseshell - the Sussex Cream we have been seeking.

If anyone has followed me thus so far, they might well ask why we didn't use the Lilac in the first place, since it would have produced both colours of Sussex with no intermediate step. This would be true in theory, but hardly practical.

As we have seen, if we are trying to isolate one pair of recessive genes (e.g., rr from Rr), there are four possible combinations, so rr will occur approximately once in every four of the progeny. This is a perfectly acceptable and practicable ratio. With two pairings (e.g., bb dd from Bd Dd) we have a one in sixteen chance, which is a much longer shot, but still within the realms of possibility; Punnet achieved it when he first produced the Normal Lilac, and it has been done many times since with similar combinations.

To go any further, though, will involve a very great increase in numbers. The Tortoiseshell and Lilac differ at three different gene locations, and their progeny would carry Bb Dd Ee. If you care to work this out, there are now eight possible combinations - eight boxes on each side of our Punnet square - and the triple recessive will occur but once in every SIXTYFOUR progeny. True, we would also get three Brown Tortoiseshells (and three Blue Tortoiseshells, or Isabellas) but this is still a lower probability than if we had done the job in two stages. The 9:3:3:1 ratio is one which occurs many times in experimental breeding, and should be taken as the maximum practical.

Anyone who is familiar with mice will know that there is a further gene which acts on melanin pigment, known as 'pink-eyed dilution'. This is nothing to do with albinism, or the ruby eye of the Havana, but a separate gene which can be inherited together with B, b, D and d. It has given rise to many very attractive pastel shades in the mouse - Dove and Champagne to name but two - and, like many of the colour genes, is also known in other species. So far, it has never been recorded in the rabbit, even in laboratory stock, although there is no scientific reason why the mutation should not occur. Possibly, in the future, the genetic engineers will be able to transplant the gene, and open up an entirely new vista for our fancy (or more grist to the mill of the "too many colours already" brigade)!

In the meantime, should anyone come across a funny-coloured rabbit with red or pink eyes, I and many others would be very pleased to hear about it.

THE COLOURS OF REX

In this section, we will look at the standards for each individual colour, with explanations and amplification if necessary.

I have taken them in the sequence in which they appear in the BRC's current book of standards, even if in some cases this means that some colours are assigned to sections to which, genetically, they do not belong.

Thus, the first section of the standards covers the self colours, those of which are (or should be) the same colour all over. Perversely, the first one is the Ermine – which has no visible colour, can in fact be self, agouti, shaded, tan-patterned or even marked as far as the rest of its genes are concerned, but as these are all masked by the double dose of albinism we can only judge it by what we see, a self white rabbit.

Ermine Rex buck, bred by Kenjim

SELF COLOURS

The Ermine
"As pure a white as possible, creamy or yellow tinge a fault".

The first point to note is that there is no mention in the standard of the eye colour; in theory this could be brown, blue or pink as long as both eyes are the same. Whilst there is, to my knowledge, at least one well-known breeder attempting to perfect the blue-eyed version, for all practical purposes Ermines have pink or red eyes: they are, in fact, albinos and can carry any other colour genes hidden, which can cause some surprises if used as an outcross!

As albinos, it might be expected that all Ermines would be pure white as the standard demands, since their genes prevent the formation of any pigments. However, if you look at a large class of Ermines on the judging table, you will see as many variations in colour as in any other variety. Some of this can be put down to the preparation of the animals – or lack of it – but there is one factor which can cause yellowing in the apparent colour of an Ermine as it ages, and that is the colour of its fat.

All rabbits, of course, lay down fat as they mature, and this is generally white in colour; sometimes, however, the fat contains residues of pigment from the food it has consumed which gives it a yellowish tinge, which will show through the skin of a white rabbit and give a pronounced yellow cast to the appearance of the coat above the layer of fat. It is almost certain that this tendency is inherited as a simple recessive gene, so the most practical advice is not to breed from any animal which turns yellowish with age, or from its parents.

That factor apart, however, the biggest influence on the colour of an Ermine is dirt. Such things as urine or beetroot stains are obvious, but the biggest enemy is dust, and people have been known to go to fantastic lengths to keep this away from the Ermines which they wanted to show. Hutches gloss-painted on the insides and washed weekly. Shredded white paper as bedding. Hay washed before feeding, and fed through external hoppers. Food sieved and vacuumed to remove the dust.

In days gone by, all exhibitors of Ermines would insist on being penned on the top tier; and many would wash their pens before letting their rabbits anywhere near them. One very prominent fancier will not even breed from any doe which does not confine its toilet activities to one corner of the hutch, which can then readily be cleaned out every day. He reckons that they will bring up their youngsters to do the same – and he could well be right.

Whilst some of the above measures may be a little extreme they give the lie to the overworked assertion that winning with white rabbits is easy: breeding them may present fewer problems, but to put one down in good show condition is a work of art.

Having said all that, it remains a fact that over the years the Ermine has been numerically the strongest of the rexes, and the most successful. The treatment of breeding and resting stock need be no different than for other colours, but those which have show potential require something different.

Whilst it is not possible to select for colour at the baby coat stage, those specimens which look the most promising for type, coat length and density should be sorted out as soon as possible and put into separate hutches.

Shredded paper may be difficult to obtain, but dust-free white wood shavings can be bought, and a very thick layer of these will be needed on the floor. Hopefully, the rabbit will only dirty one corner of the hutch, in which case a daily clean out will be possible; otherwise, the entire hutch must be cleaned one or two times a week.

The whole object of the exercise is to KEEP the animal clean: if allowed to become dirty, to GET it clean is a very difficult task, and you may well ruin it in the process. Hay can be shaken and blown to be reasonably dust-free, and tied in a bundle to the outside of the hutch, rather than put on the floor to get wet and dirty. Greenfoods must only be given in such small quantities as will be cleared up straight away, whilst roots like carrots and beetroot are best avoided altogether. Bottle drinkers are obviously an advantage compared with open dishes, but do keep an eye on the valves as a leak can quickly undo all your good work.

However clean the animal's living quarters, it is unrealistic to expect to be able to take an Ermine straight from its hutch to the show pen, as with some other breeds. There must be some dust in the atmosphere which will adhere to the oils in the rabbit's coat, and inevitably some staining of the feet must occur however often the hutch is cleaned.

The stains must be dealt with as soon as they are seen; methylated spirits or witchhazel will usually deal with them, or there are proprietary substances on the market which claim to be even more effective. The feet should be dried off, and rubbed over with one of the chalk blocks so beloved by dog fanciers. It is not a bad idea to keep the feet well chalked anyway, as staining materials will generally adhere to the chalk in preference to the rabbit's fur. Just prior to the show the entire coat should be dusted with talc, french chalk or a commercial cleaning powder sold for the purpose. This will remove the dust from the fur without damaging its natural oils. Please remember, though, that every trace of cleaning agent must be removed before the animal is penned, otherwise the judge is quite entitled to disqualify it.

For as long as Ermines have been shown, rumours have abounded that certain very successful exhibitors had their own 'secret formula' to turn a creamy rabbit into a pure white one, and at the same time improve its coat.

Let us be quite clear that if the rabbit is genetically faulty, there is nothing we can do to improve matters. On the other hand, there are several chemicals which will remove every trace of dust from the coat and make it look whiter than it was, but at the same time they remove the coat's natural oils, and spoil its appearance and texture. The oils will be replaced naturally in due course, but, in theory at least, they could be replaced by artificial means, with something which does indeed make the coat feel denser.

Such a practice, even if effective, is strictly illegal and would be most severely dealt with by any judge who detected it. To anyone who has ever actually tried improving nature in this way, let me just say this: you may well get some short-term gain, even get some misguided satisfaction that you have made such-and-such a judge look a fool. In the long term, such activities will get you absolutely nowhere. Your stock will do no good if sold to anyone else, unless you pass on the 'secret formula', and once you do that your sins will surely be visited upon you. It may be permissible to 'trim away' faults in pigeons, poultry or even dogs, but the rabbit must be shown as nature intended it.

Having said that, there is no evidence that illegal preparation is at all common among Ermines, but what is indisputable is that, on average, they do have much better coats than the other colours, and the same is true for the albino versions of many other breeds of rabbit. Is this just a coincidence, or do albinos have some inbuilt advantage when it comes to selective breeding for improvement?

There have been many theories advanced over the years, perhaps the most common being that, as colour is not a problem, the breeder is able to concentrate purely upon coat and type. There must be at least a grain of truth in this: although, as we have seen, there is a genetic factor controlling the APPARENT colour of the animal it appears far less complex than the factors governing other colours, so selective breeding for colour is accomplished more quickly and effectively with an albino.

A second theory is a little more scientific, in that it has been suggested that because the fur is white, the animal would tend to radiate more heat than a dark coloured one, and therefore needs to grow a thicker coat to compensate. An attractive theory on the surface; it is a well known fact that white-painted vehicles and aircraft remain cooler internally in tropical conditions than do dark-painted ones. However, this is due to their reflecting the radiation from the sun, and we do not, if we know what's good for them, keep our rabbits in the sun. Body heat is generally lost by convection, not radiation, and the theory is confounded by the fact that, after the Ermines, the best rex coats are carried by Blacks and Seals.

Another theory is entirely my own, and, as such, is liable to be shot down in flames the day after publication, but be that as it may!

It is known that the density of a rabbit's coat is dependent upon the number of hair follicles in the skin, a factor controlled by heredity, but not all the follicles are actually growing hair at any one time. Whilst the rabbit may be genetically capable of producing, say, a thousand hairs per square inch, it may, in practice only produce five hundred.

In the past, this difference was held to be due to purely environmental concerns; certainly, a rabbit kept in very cold conditions

will have a much denser coat than the one it will moult into if it is moved into a greenhouse. This applies whatever the colour of the animal, it will respond to environmental pressures provided that:-
a) It has the genetic potential to do so.
b) It is able to synthesise the necessary proteins to manufacture the extra hair.

As will be seen in the chapters on genetics, the metabolism of proteins is fundamental to the life-cycle. Not only is hair a protein, but so are the pigments which give the rabbit its colour.

It seems logical to me that, if two rabbits were genetically identical apart from the fact that one had genes which required it to produce pigment proteins, and the other did not (i.e. was an albino), and they were kept in identical environments, then the coloured one would have that much less protein available for the production of hair, and would be less dense that the albino. Food for thought?

For whatever reason, the Ermine was, and remains, the colour 'most likely to succeed'. It has had its ups and downs over the years, and at the present moment it must be said that it is at rather a low point, both in terms of numbers and quality; to be fair, the same might be said of many other colours. Prevalent faults must include length and texture of coat – far too many have coats which are nearly three-quarters of an inch long, with too many projecting guard hairs. Type in many cases leaves much to be desired; the bold heads and eyes of yesteryear now seem to be at a premium, whilst narrow shoulders and an unsightly dewlap spoil many an otherwise good specimen. One of the biggest problems I find is with the front feet, very often almost completely devoid of fur.

On the credit side, none of the faults are universal, so the gene pool is still there, and the specialist club is in very good hands. More than any other colour, the Ermine presents a challenge to one's showmanship and stockmanship, and as such will always be at or near the top of the popularity list.

The Black
"A rich, lustrous blue-black, dark blue undercolour carried down to the skin, brown tinge a fault. White toenails a serious fault."
At the time of writing, the Black is probably the most common

rex seen in the show pen, and has scored some notable B.I.S. awards. How strange to recall, then, that this popularity is of fairly recent origin: throughout the 'boom' years of World War Two and shortly afterwards the Black was a rarity indeed. Whatever the reason, it was not until 1950 that sufficient interest was found to form a Specialist Club; since that time, the colour has made steady, sometimes spectacular progress, interspersed with periods when certain faults became so endemic that the pundits feared a return to the A.O.V. section.

Many of the faults could have had much to do with the ancestry, as the Black was virtually remade after the war; at that time, there were quite a number of good Havanas and Blues about and these generally produced good Blacks. Some breeders, however, in the search for the ultimate in coat, used Seals and Ermines despite the strongest advice not to do so. In the case of the Seal, this resulted in the loss of the blue undercolour and a brown shade to the top colour, which can still be seen in specimens today. So bad were matters at one time that half a litter could be shown as Seals and the other half as Blacks: in one notorious case a championship was claimed for two wins as a Black and three as a Seal with the same rabbit! Needless to say, the claim was rejected, and it is doubtful if the same thing could happen today.

Nevertheless, it is true to say that the maintenance of the true blue/black top colour is the hardest aspect of breeding Blacks. It was often said in the early days that this shade of colour could not be sustained by consistent Black/Black breeding, and that an outcross to the Blue was needed every few generations. Certainly, this is a practice carried out in the Dutch and Tan fancies to good effect, but it has to be noted that a Blue Tan or Dutch is a far darker shade than the Blue Rex of today; they were definitely darker in the 1950's, and I cannot imagine that this procedure would meet with much success now.

The use of the Ermine was also frowned upon, for two reasons. Firstly, as an albino, it could and would introduce all manner of unwanted colours into the Blacks. Secondly, it was highly likely to introduce white hairs and toe nails. These were believed - correctly - to be hereditary faults carried hidden down the generations by the

Ermine, just waiting to ruin an otherwise good Black!

Whatever their origin, white hairs remain the biggest bugbear with the Black, although white toe nails seem to be a thing of the past.

White patches, of course, are a total disqualification, but it must be noted that they can stem from two different causes. They can come from a recessive gene associated with the Dutch pattern, in which case they will tend to be confined to the nose, jaw and front feet. Breeding from an animal with this sort of patch is obviously to be avoided, but if the patches are elsewhere on the body, all hope is

Black Rex, breeder unknown

not lost. Any damage to the skin of a baby rabbit at birth or shortly afterwards will destroy the pigment cells so that the fur, when it grows, will be white. In this case, it may be worth taking a risk and breeding from the rabbit, although, of course, there is no absolute guarantee that the fault is not a hereditary one, the only proof of that pudding being in the eating.

Most coloured animals will carry the odd one or two white hairs; these are generally guard hairs, and most breeders would pull them out as and when they are spotted with no-one being any the wiser. A word of warning, however: apart from the dubious legality of this procedure, the white hairs will always grow through again; if you accidentally pull out some of the adjacent hairs in the process of removing the white one, then they will also come through white. So, what was a small fault can easily be transformed into a bigger one, or even a disqualification.

The very worst type of white hairs are those which are carried in the undercoat, and can be seen to extend over most of the animal's back when the fur is parted. Quite definitely hereditary: never use an animal with this fault for breeding. It is surprising, though, how many judges fail to spot them!

Type and coat in the Black are, generally speaking, as good as will be found in any rex, possibly the worst aspect being the occasional over-large dewlap. Very often, this will be liberally sprinkled with white hairs, and is not a pretty sight, but in the main present day Blacks are as good as they ever have been, a credit to breeders past and present.

Mrs K Warner's Blue Rex doe, winner at the 1979 Bradford Ch Show

The Blue

"Clear, bright, medium shade of blue (not lavender) throughout, from tip of fur to skin, extending to, but not including toenails, brown tinge a fault. Toenails to be horn colour, white toenails to be treated as a minor fault."

This somewhat lengthy description still does not adequately convey the delicate pastel shade of a good Blue. An actual blue pigment does not, of course, occur in mammals, only varying shades of grey and the one we are looking for is just a shade darker than the foliage of the lavender plant. Anything lighter will be a fault according to the standard, whereas the darker shades show a marked tendency towards darker extremities and, very often, a pronounced brownish tinge, which would be an even bigger fault.

There seems to be no general agreement in the rabbit fancy as to what the medium shade of blue should be: a Dutch should be as deep a tint as possible, whilst the Tan standard calls for a medium shade, but in practise the Tan will be very much darker than the Dutch. All I can say is that the Blue rex should be very much lighter than either of them, without being as light as a Beveren.

In the decade after the Second World War, the Blue achieved possibly the height of its success on the show bench; the odds against a Blue being best rex were very much shorter than they are today, with many equalling the Ermine for type and coat qualities. It must be said that this was achieved only by the acceptance of a rather darker shade than we would look for now; heads, ears and feet generally were one or two shades darker than the body, whilst even the best were not free of the brownish overcast to the colour.

Whether it was the effort to lighten the colour which led to a deterioration in coat quality and a lessening in the numbers shown, is not quite clear. It does seem to be the case that the more dilute the pigment, the longer the coat, with a tendency to curl.

It is certainly true that at the moment the Blues are in too few hands, the average coat is a shade too long and particularly in youngsters, there is a noticeable curl to the coat, especially on the belly. On the opposite side of the balance, colour in general is much clearer, brighter and more level. Whilst in some cases the effect is spoiled by dark guard hairs, or by undercolour which is either paler or darker than the top, in general today's Blues are a far more attractive colour than they used to be. It is only when the rabbit is handled that the loss of coat quality becomes apparent.

Much of the improvement in colour can be attributed to what is known as the "snowball" – the one which is practically white in the nest coat and may not reach its final colour shade until it is a full adult. Whether this trait is caused by a separate primary gene, or merely an accumulation of modifiers has never been conclusively proved; what is certain is that the "snowballs" enjoy most success in the show pen.

I often wonder if, in fact, the use of these animals has been overdone. Whilst the "snowball" may make a better exhibition rabbit, they perhaps ought not to be mated together. One which has been blue from birth may well be a better long-term prospect for breeding.

The "snowball" may well be responsible for another fault which happily seems to be becoming less common, that of white toenails. A few years ago this was worrying some breeders so much that it was made a disqualification. This resulted in so many rabbits being thrown off the table that a drastic rethink became necessary. One could have spent hours listening to learned discourses as to the difference between a white toenail and a 'clear' one.

In actual fact, of course, there is no distinction. As a pigment, white does not exist, so what the people who framed the standard really mean is that the toenails must be pigmented.

This puts the "snowball" at a disadvantage as a youngster, as the toenails are invariably the last part of the rabbit to develop pigment. Many a good Blue must have been discarded as a baby which could later have become a champion. Strangely, once the standard was changed to its present wording, the problem seems to have diminished: possibly breeders have connected it to excessive reliance on "snowballs" and reduced their use.

Little more needs to be said about coats: many are quite dense, but in general they need to be shorter and less curly. If today's breeders will concentrate on this aspect, and not try to make the colour too light, then there is every prospect of this most attractive colour going right back to the top.

The Havana

"A rich dark chocolate, the colour to go well down the fur, pearl-grey undercolour to reach the skin".

A winning Havana Rex exhibited by Ray Homer

The National Havana Club was amongst the first to cater for Rex and still insists on its own version of type. Here is what we must look for in the Havana:

Shape: Compact, cobby body, short neck, broad and rounded loins, wide and well-developed hindquarters.

Head: Medium size, but not coarse, broader in bucks.

Ears: Erect and in proportion to the body.

Eyes: Same colour as body, glowing ruby red in subdued light.

Legs: Short, straight, fine in bone, brown toenails.

Thus the ideal Havana rex will be a much cobbier rabbit than any other, with a very pronounced emphasis on the development of the rear end.

The term "dark" called for in the colour standard has to be understood as a relative one: due to the shortness of coat and its being carried more or less at right angles to the skin, the best coloured rexes will never appear to be as dark as the best normals.

Probably the biggest problem is not the actual shade of the pigmentation, but the fact that it does not extend far enough down the hair shaft, a fault which shows up particularly on the belly and chest, sometimes giving the impression of a shaded rabbit. Having said that, however, there is no doubt that a good coloured Havana at its peak is a most attractive animal, which will give as good as it gets on the show bench.

Unfortunately, this colour is very prone to show signs of "rusting", particularly just before the onset of a moult. Sunshine is, of course, fatal to the colour: indeed, many breeders will take pains to keep their exhibition stock away from even normal daylight. When I had this colour, the advice was always to breed them dark and then keep them in the dark, advice which I think is very valid.

One point which has to be watched is the undercolour. This must be a fairly dark shade of grey so as not to adversely affect the overall colour and it must not show a white band next to the skin.

In terms of coat, it is probably easier to find the correct half-inch length on a Havana than on any other colour: in fact, some could be criticised for being too short, which does not do a lot for the texture, and may give the impression of a lack of density. Whilst there is a tendency in some strains to carry a lot of coarse guard-hairs, the average coat quality compares favourably with the Blacks and Ermines.

One major shortcoming seems fortunately to be now a thing of the past and that is temperament. My first rex was a Havana and for years I carried the scars to prove it.

The Lilac

"A pinkish dove-grey, even throughout, undercolour to be as near as possible to top colour. Brown or bluish tinge a fault".

A very close relative of the Blue, of course, although it has never achieved any great degree of popularity, or outstanding success at the classic shows. If the Blue is prone to suffer from long and curly coats, then so is the Lilac, but even more so!

In my early days in the fancy, it was some time before I even saw a Lilac, so rare were they, and I must admit to being distinctly under-impressed by my first sight of one. Type and size it certainly had; in the correct light it could be said that there was a slight pinky tinge to the colour, but it was very uneven - flaky perhaps describes it best, but the biggest disappointment was the coat. Nearly an inch long, no density and very woolly. This was shown by one of the leading names in Lilac-rex at the time, so it must have been typical of what was on offer: no wonder the colour was in so few hands.

What, then, of today's Lilacs? To my intense regret they must be regarded as virtually extinct; there may still be the odd specimen tucked away in some fancier's shed, but entries at shows are conspicuous by their absence. This is most galling, as there was a period when the breed appeared to be making great headway in terms of quality. Specimens of good type were quite common; coats were approaching the correct length and – very occasionally – the correct pinky-dove shade, level all over, was produced. All gone, now, apparently, for reasons I went into in an earlier chapter. Too few breeders, too small a gene pool, inbred lack of fecundity, end of story.

At its best, this is such an attractive colour that it must not be allowed to disappear. Rex breeders have never ducked a challenge, surely there are three or four fanciers willing to try to recreate the breed. I'm afraid it is a question of **recreating** it, as, even if there are any of the old strain left, we know they will not breed successfully, even if outcrossed.

There are three possible methods to consider – the first two of which can hardly be recommended. One could use the Normal, bred to a Blue or Havana Rex. Sadly, even the normals have hit hard times; they lack the size of the rex and, more importantly, they lack sufficient density. I doubt that would be a productive road down which to travel.

The second alternative would be to use the Lynx, or the Lilac Otter. The latter have hardly been seen since the standard was accepted, but I mention the possibility in case some were available. In theory, the Lynx (or Lilac Agouti) would be a good prospect. Used with Blues or Havanas, a proportion of true-breeding Lilacs would appear in the second generation.

In practice, of course, the Lynx is itself in danger of extinction, and can hardly be considered to provide a favourable gene pool. Furthermore, the suggested outcross would only produce one Lilac in sixteen births – exactly the same proportion (if you followed the chapter on genetics), as would come from the direct cross of a Blue with a Havana. Because the Blue/Havana cross is the one most likely to introduce hybrid vigour to our foundation stock, it has to be the only viable option.

We have already seen that the result of this cross is visual Blacks. The second generation would produce Blacks, Havanas, Blues and Lilacs in the (theoretical) proportions 9:3:3:1. The Havanas which I would choose would be too light in colour for showing, but as level all over as obtainable. For preference, those with an ultra short and "Hard" coat should be used, together with impeccable type and size. The Blues should be of good exhibition quality, with as little curl in the coat as possible. They will probably have been "snowballs" as youngsters, which may turn out to be an advantage in fixing the colour of the subsequent Lilacs.

There is at least five years hard work here for someone. I mentioned three or four breeders making the attempt, and it really would need to be a co-operative effort. There could be nothing worse than for the breed to be re-created in one stud, only to be wiped out by disease, inbreeding or a loss of interest on the part of the owner. Several breeders, sharing stock and ideas, would, I believe, be essential to prevent all the problems of the past rearing their ugly heads again. Viability and fecundity would have to be selected far ahead of the exhibition qualities. Any takers?

The Nutria
    "Rich golden brown, colour to go well down the fur, pearl-grey undercolour to reach the skin, rusty tinge a fault".
    This standard has been in the books for as far back as I can trace,

but I know of no-one active in the fancy today who has ever seen one. From what I gathered from the old hands, the colour was supposed to resemble the South American water rat known as the Nutria or Coypu, a shade of brown unlike any other in the rabbit fancy. When the Coypu was present in East Anglia it had a colour which would certainly have fitted the Nutria standard, but it could equally have been described as having a rusty tinge, and this is probably the reason why this colour has become extinct.

Could it be recreated? There is no equivalent colour in the Normal Fur breeds and a poor-coloured Havana rex would certainly not fit the bill. I have had these turn up in litters of Blacks and Cinnamons, but whilst they resembled milk rather than plain chocolate, they could certainly not be described as "golden" brown.

Two possibilities do come to mind, both involving the brown gene "bb". Firstly, in conjunction with dominant black "E^D".

Whilst I have no direct experience of using stock with the "E^D" gene, I see no reason why it should not act with "bb" as well as "BB", but intuition tells me that the shade of brown produced would be more likely to be even darker than the Havana.

The other possibility is the gene which converts black pigment to a sepia shade – c^{chl} c^{chl} – as found in the Seal. It could be expected to have a lightening effect on brown pigment and might well result in the desired golden tint.

Technically, this would be a shaded rabbit, of course, but it is a well-known fact that if Seals are bred together for several generations there is a very strong possibility that the shadings will be bred out, resulting in what to the naked eye is a self-coloured animal. I offer this as the most likely origin of the Nutria and it should be relatively simple for anyone interested enough to try and produce it to do so by crossing a Havana and a Seal. The F1 generation would be all Blacks and the F2's would result in 9 Blacks, 3 Havanas, 3 Seals to every Nutria produced - if Nutria they indeed are. However, whether with the standard as at present worded it would be a worthwhile exercise is a different matter: what to me is a golden shade might easily be described as rusty.

I have every sympathy with those who are trying to recreate the old breeds and produce new ones; I have done it myself and will continue to do so, but as far as producing a golden brown rabbit without a rusty tinge to it is concerned, I have other brick walls to bang my head against!

SHADED VARIETIES

Smoke Pearl - Siamese
"COLOUR: saddle smoke-grey shading to pearl-grey on flanks, chest and belly. Head, ears, feet and upper side of tail to match saddle as nearly as possible. Shading to be gradual, avoiding blotches or streaks. General undercolour to match shading as closely as possible. To be totally free from white hairs throughout. Toe nails horn coloured.
   TYPE: neat with moderate length of body. Head: medium size, broader in bucks. Ears: erect and in proportion to body; well furred.
   EYES: bright and bold with distinct ruby glow.
   FAULTS: pale or white undercolour."
   Until comparatively recently, Smoke Pearl rexes were little better than shorter coated versions of their normal counterpart. Tending to be on the dark side, their worst fault was a long, sometimes woolly coat, very often with a profusion of guard hairs.
   A determined effort has now been made by a few dedicated

Siamese Smoke Pearl Rex bred by Syd Gilliard

enthusiasts to improve matters, and I believe that one or two have used the Sable with what appears to be success. However it has been achieved, there is no doubt that the best of today's Smokes can hold their own against most other colours in terms of coat, whilst colour has improved out of all recognition. Only some rather snipey heads need to be bred out to bring the type up to scratch.

Whereas in the past the colour could have been described as more smoke than pearl, this is rarely the case now: flanks, chest and belly have attained a really delicate shade of pearl grey, with very level shadings down from the saddle.

If any criticism at all is to be levelled, it might be said that the saddles are not dark enough when compared to the points: they are certainly rather difficult to discern on some specimens, and one or two are definitely too light in the nape region.

On the other hand, if the saddle is darker then the pearl grey shadings will not become evident until the lower parts of the flank are reached and much of the attraction is lost. Whilst there must be a definite saddle, I think breeders should try to produce the points to match it rather than the other way round.

As a derivative of the Sable, the big problem with the Smokes is that they do not breed true: on average, only half the litter will be of potential show colour, the rest being albinos and dark slate greys.

In theory, of course, the albinos and slate-greys could be mated together to produce all exhibition-type colour; those who have tried it have found that it doesn't always work, and they still produce albinos and slate greys in every litter! The only reason I can think of is that the slate-grey used was not dark enough! Instead of having the genetic constitution $C^{chl} C^{chl}$ it must have been $C^{chl} c$ plus modifiers to make it appear as dark as the dominant slate variety.

The analogy with the Sable and Seal is valid: Sable/Sable matings will invariably produce 50% Sables, 25% albinos and 25% Seals. However, the modifying genes will act upon the Sables to either lighten or darken the colour, and may possibly make it so dark that to all intents and purposes the animal is a Seal. Only a test mating to an albino bred from Sables would prove the matter - if just one albino turns up in the litter than the apparent Seal was, in fact, a Sable.

However, that is not the main reason for not using the albino/ slate mating, other than for curiosity's sake. How can you tell whether the albino carries the genes for white hairs? How can you tell whether the slate rabbit carried genes for good shadings? If I were consistently breeding well-shaded rabbits with no sign of white hairs, but my average litter size were small, then I might well be tempted, but not otherwise.

Siamese Sable

"Saddle an even rich sepia brown, shading gradually to a chestnut on flanks and slightly paler on belly. Head, ears, legs and upper side of tail to match saddle. Chest to match flanks. Top colour to go well down fur, undercolour to match shadings throughout. Eye colour to reflect a distinct rich ruby glow.

FAULTS: Streaks or blotches, white hairs, rusty tinge, white toe nails."

A Sable of the correct colour, in full coat, is an impressive sight, carrying a sheen not apparent on many other colours. The saddle will extend in an unbroken line from the nape to the tail, and the hallmark of a good specimen is when you cannot tell where the saddle ends and the shadings begin - an imperceptible merging is what is required. The flanks will carry a rich chestnut sheen, setting off the darker points, and the ruby glow to the eyes is really distinct. To breed such an animal is an achievement in itself: to keep it in that state is another matter entirely.

With some colours, a slight degree of moult is only apparent on close examination, but with the Sable the slightest trace will play havoc with the shadings, resulting in the streaks and blotches which, if we are honest, can be found on most show stock. The old fur, before it falls out, will become several shades lighter, often taking on a rusty hue, whilst the new fur, before it achieves its final length, will be much darker than its final shade.

It follows, therefore, that the primary aim in setting up a strain of Sables is to produce stock which moults quickly and cleanly, otherwise your perfect specimen will only be in its prime on the one day in the year when there is no show to go to!

Siamese Sable exhibited by Claret & Gold, Bradford Ch Show 2001

One factor which is sometimes missing in the colour equation is the rich chestnut shade on the flanks; all too often these are more of a milk chocolate shade which, whilst it has a certain attraction, is not what the standard calls for. Only selective breeding will correct this tendency, and it may well be necessary to keep stock, purely for breeding, which carries the correct richness of colour even if they themselves are either too light or dark overall for show.

The standard itself makes no distinction between light, medium or dark shades, although they all exist, as they do with the Normal Sables. The really dark rexes are known as Seals, which we will cover next. At one time there was a standard for the Dark Sable as well but, rightly or wrongly, this has been deleted. The really light shades will tend to have an indistinct saddle and be much too light on the belly, so we can take it as read that the medium is the truly correct shade for exhibition.

It is, however, the rabbit fancy's version of Murphy's Law that these animals will not breed true; as discussed in the chapter on colour inheritance, the medium shades invariably carry one albino gene. Without this gene the animal is a Seal, with two it is an Ermine, so that only fifty per cent of any litter are liable to be Sables. Whilst the albinos are not likely to be of any practical use, the Seals certainly are, both for show and breeding.

Much of the variation in colour between fairly dark and light is caused by modifying genes, and it is entirely possible that a strain could be evolved which bred every shade between a fairly dark medium and a fairly light Seal, without producing any albinos.

It is, however, likely that neither the Seals nor the Sables produced would really be the ideal shade, and the most profitable course is that adopted by most breeders, which is to breed Sable to Seal if not continuously, then about every third generation. This process will eliminate the albino, and the progeny will average half Sables and half Seals, so they all start off with an equal chance of making show standard.

If, for any reason, you want to rear only Sables in a litter, they can be quite easily spotted when the babies are about three days old. Seals will look almost black, albinos pink and the Sable will be a silvery shade, which it will take several weeks to lose. So, although you can tell that the rabbit will be a Sable from its very early stages, it will be a long time before you can assess its shadings.

We have already discussed most of the potential faults: streaks and blotches are more often due to changing coats than to inherent breeding faults. Too distinct a demarcation between saddle and flank colour – known as abrupt shadings – is a different matter and can very easily be bred into a strain. The undercolour on the saddle should be a definite sepia shade, not a milk chocolate or slate grey colour; neither of those shades will give the beautiful chestnut on the flanks. As the standard states, the undercolour should become paler as the top colour lightens down the sides, but not too pale.

White toe nails are, fortunately, rarely seen. The next stage is a completely white toe, which is a disqualification, of course, so never breed from a rabbit with any white claws.

White hairs are slightly different: most non-agouti rexes carry the odd white hair if you look closely enough, and should not detract too much from an otherwise good animal. Very pronounced white streaks, whilst ruining the rabbit for show, are most likely to have been caused by damage at birth, and need not prevent the use of the animal for breeding.

The white hairs you really need to worry about are those which can only be seen in the undercoat when the fur is parted: never, ever, breed from a Sable (or any other rex) like this; it is one of the easiest faults to breed in, and impossible to breed out.

Seal

"Head and body an even rich dark sepia, shading only slightly paler on lower flanks, chest and belly. Top colour to go well down fur, undercolour to match shadings throughout. Eye colour to reflect deep bluish black. Faults: uneven top colour, rusty tinge, white toe nails, white hairs; blue undercolour a serious fault."

Strictly speaking we should call this rabbit the Siamese Seal, to distinguish it from the Marten, but it has not yet become the custom, and probably will not unless, and until, the Martens become more numerous.

As we have seen, the Seal is really a Dark Sable, can be bred from Sables and – almost always – just has the edge when it comes to density. Both breeds have inherited from their Normal forbears an excellent texture to the coat and both are generally of good type, but whether you are sorting out a litter, or judging a class at a show, nine times out of ten the best Seals will be denser than the best Sables.

The same thing happens in the normals, the Darks almost invariably winning on coat, and I can offer no explanation; the only difference between the two colours is that the Sable generally carries one albino gene, but this might be expected to make the coat more dense if it has any effect at all. It is a fact of life: the Sable is the one to look at and admire, but the Seal is the one which will do the winning!

That is not to say that the Seal is not an attractive rabbit in its own right, because it is. The sepia shade is very subtle – very dark, but definitely not black, and several degrees lighter underneath without a visible demarcation line or any hint of rustiness. Because of the normally excellent coats, the Seals can be expected to be in contention for the major awards; there are no major drawbacks either to their breeding or nurture, and all in all they are a good variety for the novice to choose, always bearing in mind that the competition is

N Croft's Seal, best Rex at Bradford Ch Show 1974

that much stronger than it would be with some of the less popular breeds.

The other advantage that the Seal has over the Sable is that two Seals can be bred together and produce nothing but Seals, giving one that much wider a choice in the litters. However, it has to be said that this is not the normal method of breeding. Try as one may to avoid it, after two or three successive Seal/Seal bred generations, most of the shadings will have disappeared, together with the major attraction of the breed. Although the difficulty of getting and keeping the Sable in full coat may deter you from showing them, you must keep one or two to breed from.

There have been times when the average Seal was so dark that it was almost impossible to distinguish it from a Black – indeed at one time the standard included the words 'almost black'. This only served to encourage indiscriminate cross-breeding, to the detriment of both colours. The offending phrase has now been deleted and a serious fault made of blue undercolour, so no longer can a rabbit be shown as a Seal one week and a Black the next. In actual fact, the undercolour on a good Seal will have a definite yellow tinge to it, reflecting the fact that the top colour is brown and not black.

Most of the other faults mentioned are common to Seals and Sables and have already been covered. An uneven top colour and/ or a rusty tinge may be an inbred fault, but much more likely to be caused by incipient moult; although the Seal must be expected to moult in the same way as a Sable, it will tend not to show the effects to such a drastic extent, and so will have a rather longer show life.

When I had the breed myself, I found that I had problems with bare hocks, but I put that down to the particular strain I had; there is no evidence that it is a general problem with the breed, which remains one of the most successful of the rexes.

The Tortoiseshell

"Top colour (saddle) to be rich orange, going well down towards the skin and lightly tipped with brown; ears, muzzle, feet, belly and underside of tail to be rich blue-black, gradually shading into the body colour on face, flanks and haunches."

Although it is a shaded-self rabbit like the Seals, Sables and Smoke Pearls, the Tortoiseshell is in no way related to them. In fact, of course, the shadings are caused by an entirely different factor, and go in the opposite direction, the rabbit being darker underneath than on the back.

I have been given the credit for the introduction of this breed, although there is evidence to suggest that it was being kept, if not exhibited, as long ago as 1947, whereas mine did not appear until 1978. If any credit is due to me it is for the standardisation of the variety, a course I was forced into by ambiguities in the general standard which have still not been satisfactorily sorted out. The standard is a bit of a "hotch-potch", being a distillation of the six or more descriptions of the colour which already existed for other breeds.

The top colour must be as rich and bright an orange as possible, and only very lightly "dusted" with brown ticking. Too heavy a ticking will result in a very dull top colour, which gets worse as the animal

Gwen Soutar's Tortoiseshell Rex, Bradford Ch Show 1999

gets older, so a young Tortoiseshell should have as little ticking as possible. Although there is no mention of undercolour in the standard it will be a creamy-white, and the less of it the better, ideally the orange will reach almost to the skin.

The standard for the colour of the shadings, culled from standards relating to Normal Fur and Fancy breeds, calls for a blue-black shade, which has yet to be achieved. Most of the intensity of the shadings in the other breeds comes from the guard hairs which the rex does not have, and our shadings are really of a sepia tone. Whether it will ever be possible to produce the same type of shadings as can be found on the Thuringer only time can tell. It is tempting to suggest changing the standard, which has not been revised since its acceptance in 1981, but that would probably only result in someone finally producing the blue-black shade only to find it was now a fault! After all, the points on a Himalayan should be black, but in reality are sepia, and that standard was set in the last century.

When I said that my Tortoiseshells "appeared" in 1978 I meant the term literally. Having worked out many years previously how they might be produced, the time and conditions never seemed quite right to actually set about doing so, and the first three actually turned up in a litter of Castors. Inbred to start with, and considerably more so by the time three generations of pure-bred stock had been produced, that strain did not last long and any links today's rabbits have with the original ones are tenuous to say the least.

Problems? The biggest difficulty now appears to be stabilising the colour. The points in particular seem to lose their intensity as the rabbit gets older, and that, coupled with the tendency for the top colour to darken with age can result in one's breeding stock looking a dirty brown colour all over. On the other hand, there are not that many colours in rex which can be successfully shown beyond their first birthday, so we are really no worse off than anyone else.

Coats have improved since the early days, although, as with most breeds, there is room for further improvement. Type and size at this point in time are well up to standard.

All in all, although this breed has its problems, and possibly a standard which can never be achieved, it is in no worse shape than many older-established rexes. What is really needed now is for someone to start again from square one, with really first-class Blacks and Oranges as a foundation. That way we would certainly get better coats and, who knows, real blue-black shadings which last.

TAN PATTERNED REX

Marten Sable Rex bred by Bernard Welford

Marten Sable & Marten Seal

In both these varieties, the standard for saddle and flank colour is the same as that for the Siamese. The belly, eye circles, inside of ears, underside of jowl and nape triangle to be white. The listed faults are also the same as for the Siamese, with the added faults of white hairs on outside of ears and on body and white ticking on flanks or rump. The standard for the Marten Sable states that white ticking on legs is permissible, but the Seal standard makes no mention of this.

The real question with both the standards is what is meant by 'ticking'? In the Normal version, the ticking comprises longer than normal guard hairs, and any rex (apart from the Fox) which carries protruding guard hairs will be faulted.

However, provided that the white hairs which exist as part of the pattern do not protrude above the surface of the fur, most judges would not penalise the rabbit, but accept it as the normal state of affairs. This is particularly true in the case of the chest, which is invariably a mixture of white and sepia hairs.

Likewise, the division between the flanks and belly colour: do

Marten Seal Rex bred by Miss M Dodds

we want a straight demarcation line, with no white in the sepia, or is a merging of the two colours permissible? There are certainly some anomalies in these standards which need clarifying if the Marten rexes are to achieve the same relative popularity as their Normal counterparts.

As mentioned in the discussion of the Smoke Pearl, the Marten ought to enjoy a built-in advantage over the Siamese pattern, in that there is no problem with uneven shadings or white hairs on the belly. To some extent this is true in practise, and there have been some very good Martens produced in recent years. Strangely, most of these have been Seals; the Marten Sable, although a most attractive creature, is much rarer than the Seal.

Martens and Siamese can be bred together, and often are. The Marten pattern is dominant, so there is no reason why greater numbers of Martens cannot be bred and shown.

Two final points: a white belly is much easier to produce than a shaded one, but it must be WHITE, not slate-blue with a little white tipping to the hairs, as we see too often.

The Marten pattern will obviously mask any white hairs carried in the patterned areas, so do be careful not to introduce this fault into the Siamese when breeding the two patterns together.

The Orange

"**Saddle deep rich orange carried well down the sides gradually shading to white belly. Colour to go well down the fur, undercolour to be white. Eye circles, inside of ears and underside of jowl white. Chest to match flanks. Face and outside ears to match saddle. FAULTS: Ticking, barred front feet and brownish tinge, blue undercolour.**"

Here we have a rabbit with shadings, classed as Tan-Pattern but which is, in fact, an Agouti! The reasons for this date back to the very early days of the breed, when it was felt that the Orange could not really compete with the Lynxes, Castors and Chinrex, so

Cyril Ridgeway: only breeder to date to have achieved best Rex at Bradford Ch Show with an Orange

they were put into a category which, at the time, was virtually unoccupied. So much has the Orange improved since those early days that it would probably now dominate the Agouti section were it to be transferred.

This improvement is of comparatively recent origin; the Orange does not seem to have shared in the boom period of the War. Despite having two specialist clubs (one of which also catered for Fawns), the breed remained something of an exotic rarity until the two clubs amalgamated.

Then for a time, during the 1960's and 70's, the popularity of the Orange was almost equal to the Ermines and Blacks; whether the quality kept pace is another question. I think that most of us who were showing and judging during that period would have to admit that, whilst some of the best were of a very high standard, the average quality left something to be desired.

Even the best, although some really excelled in colour, tended to be rather long in coat, and needed more density. Thus, they tended not to figure very highly in the duplicate classes, even though in some cases they accounted for half the rex entries.

Now, of course, the boom years are over, and the numbers of Orange shown represent what is probably just a slight improvement on earlier figures. What has to be said, in all fairness, is that those breeders who have stayed with the variety through good times and bad are now producing stock with such improved coats that they can compete against the other colours without any "pushing".

With some breeds, the name is practically meaningless. With the Orange, it says it all! The aim is a "Jaffa" shade, and many achieve this, at least along the back; where a lot fail is in not carrying this colour far enough down the sides, which should, and can, be almost as rich a colour as the saddle.

Others are practically level all over, without carrying the essential richness and depth of colour. The object of the exercise is to marry the two types together, and one or two have done just that. The most likely route to success is to concentrate on reducing the extent of the undercolour; the further down the hair shaft the top colour goes, the better the overall effect must be.

The standard does not call for any exact proportion of undercolour, and I have found that the ones with the best colour are invariably those with the least undercolour. It does not matter how little of it there is, as long as it is white and not blue.

Blue undercolour, in itself, does not have any effect on the picture as a whole. The reason why it is undesirable is that it goes hand-in-hand with dark ticking on ears and rump. Eliminate one fault and the other will usually go with it.

In some cases, a blue tinge to the undercolour is caused by moult:

the skin itself looks blue where the new hair is growing, and this will be reflected on the fur. If a rabbit which is not about to moult shows blue undercolour, it is best avoided.

Barred front feet, although they have always been listed as a fault, were never very prevalent even in the boom years; of late, however, we do seem to be getting more of them. This is a fault which ought to be bred out now, while there is still enough unaffected stock to choose from.

As I have mentioned, by determined efforts, some breeders are now turning out Oranges with short, nicely textured coats which almost, if not quite, match up to the best of the other varieties.

I think it is no coincidence that, as the coat has become shorter, the band of undercolour has narrowed, and the overall colour has improved. It has been my pleasure to put up an Orange for the highest honours more than once in the last few years, and I hope to have many more opportunities to do so.

The Fox
"Black: Colour jet black, colour to go well down the fur. Undercolour to be as dark blue as possible. Eye circles, inside ears, line of jaws, underside of tail and belly, to be pure white, with undercolour permissible. Triangle to be white and as small as possible. White ticking on chest, flanks and rump desirable. Ticking may protrude beyond fur as in Normal Foxes, such ticking to be white tipped hairs and to be considered an added beauty. Eyes brown or grey, brown preferred."
FAULTS: Rusty tinge, pale undercolour.
DISQUALIFICATION: Yellow or other colour in white pattern.
BLUE: A medium blue (even and sound), extending to the skin. Eyes blue or grey, blue preferred.

CHOCOLATE: Dark chocolate (even and sound), top colour going down the fur as far as possible. Undercolour slate. Eyes brown or lilac, brown preferred.

LILAC: Pinky-dove top colour (even and sound). Undercolour dove. Eyes lilac with ruby glow."

J Watson's Black Fox, exhibited at the 2000 Southern Ch Show

Many readers will, I know, never have seen a Fox-rex. They would be as surprised as I was once to learn that, in the opinion of most of the leading judges of the time, the nearest to perfection in a post-war rex was a Fox.

Never very numerous, they tended to exist only in isolated pockets, rather than being spread around the country. I was fortunate to live in one of these areas, the records showing that one J Hodgkiss attained the dizzy heights of V.H.C. in the Fox class at the Northants Rex Y.S.S. in 1952; number in class, eight - perhaps the other three didn't turn up! As fanciers tended not to travel very far afield in those days, you could have lived just thirty miles from Northampton and not realised that the breed existed.

Despite the excellence of that one particular rabbit, it has to be said that the breed suffered from a number of faults. They must have been produced comparatively recently from the Normal, so that the coats, although fairly dense, carried a lot of guard hairs. They could be, and were, produced in all four colours, but only the Black had an official standard, so one took one's chances in showing the other colours.

Probably the biggest obstacle the Fox had to overcome was the lack of unanimity regarding the ticking: the only reference to ticking in the standard of that time was that it should not be excessive, which left the field wide open to a number of different interpretations.

Some judges wanted just a patterned rabbit, with a straight demarcation between flank and belly colour; an attractive enough rabbit, but hardly a Fox. Others wanted ticking, but regarded anything above the surface of the fur as guard hairs and penalised it as such.

Yet another school of thought recognised that ticking must protrude, but the general coat should not carry guard hairs.

This is the view which eventually prevailed, and was embodied into today's standard: unfortunately, by the time this was done, the Fox had virtually disappeared from the scene.

This is, at its best, a most attractive variety which should be capable of being bred to a very high standard. If anyone wanted to start up completely from scratch, there are three possible avenues to explore: to stay within the rex breeds either the Marten or the Otter could be used, or one could go to the ultimate extreme and go back to the Normal Fox.

Taking the Marten alternative first, the objective is to replace the "light chinchillation" gene (C^{chl} C^{chl}) with that for "dark chinchillation" (C^{chd} C^{chd}). This gene is carried by the Chinrex, so the first course will be to cross Marten Seal with Chinrex. (I would not advise the Marten Sable, otherwise albinism will be introduced).

The F1 progeny will look like Chinrex, possibly rather dark, but almost certainly with really dense coats: please don't try to sell these as Chinrex, however good they look; they are purely experimental stock for your own use. Mate them together, and out of every sixteen youngsters you should get nine Chins, three very light Chins known as 'ghosts', three Foxes and one Marten Seal.

Of any Foxes produced, two-thirds will carry the "light chinchillation" gene as a recessive, and so will be expected to produce twenty-five percent Martens in their litters. As it will almost certainly be at least three generations before the correct top colour can be established in the Foxes, this cross may well produce a great deal of stock which could be taken for a dark Marten or a poor coloured Fox.

Thus it is probably not to be recommended unless test-matings on all apparent Foxes are carried out first. This could be achieved by using an albino bred from Sables; any Foxes carrying the "light-chinchillation" gene will, mated to this albino, produce a proportion of Sables, which can be recognised at a very early age. The great advantage of the Marten cross is that coats should be expected to be of high quality from the word go.

Turning to the possibilities which the Otter offers, this should again be crossed with a Chinrex, but in this case the F1 generation will look like Castors. Out of every sixteen in the F2 litters, nine will be Castors, three Chins, three Otters and one Fox. Thus, this cross will produce fewer Foxes, but they will not carry the recessives which the Marten will introduce; any Foxes produced will be known to be true breeding, without need of test-mating.

The major disadvantage to using either the Marten or Otter rex is that neither variety carries ticking, or at least not in the profusion required by the current standard for Fox-rex. To get this ticking I can really see no alternative to using the normal Fox, with all its attendant problems. These must include:- a loss of density; loss of size; poor texture and excessive guard hairs. None of these problems are insurmountable, fortunately, provided that the correct foundation stock is used.

The first criterion must be size; there are many who would hold that today's Foxes are too big, so this is not an impossible objective! You need something which weighs at least seven pounds, more if possible; if a doe, make sure its dewlap is in proportion, many fail in this respect.

Secondly, your eventual requirement is ticking on your rexes, so make sure your stock has ticking in abundance; many young Foxes are ticked practically all over, and lose a lot of it as they mature, so make sure that what you buy is not going to get worse as it gets older.

The third, and most difficult factor will be the type of coat, of which there are several. One is rather long, soft and silky, and will do you no good at all. The ideal exhibition type coat in the Fox will again be rather long, with a good flow to it, and ticking which is much longer than the rest of the guard hairs. Whilst better (and inevitably more expensive) than the first type, it is still not ideal as it would almost certainly lead to your rexes being long in coat, with too many guard hairs. The third type has a much shorter coat, with roll-back tendencies, and ticking which only just protrudes above the surface. They also tend to be dense, which accounts for the number which get shown, although they do not really fit the Normal Fox standard. For our purposes, they would be ideal, and you might even be able to borrow some, as you will only need to produce the one F1 generation from them.

The rex to choose might, at first sight, seem to be the Black, since what we are trying to do is put a white pattern onto a black rabbit, and the Black is one of the highest quality rexes we have. The Black Rex/Silver Fox cross would indeed produce Fox-rex, but only in the proportion of 3:64 in the F2 generation and would not breed true; refer back to the chapter on heredity and you will see that there are differences at three gene loci, whereas it is possible to use a cross where only two relevant genes differ, reducing the odds to 1:16, which are quite long enough!

There are really only two practical choices, the Chinrex or the Otter; I would go for the Chin. Whilst perhaps not carrying quite the density of the best of the Blacks, the coats on many Chinrex are more than adequate; very often one can find a rather dark specimen, very narrow in the pearl, but with ideal density and length of coat. It will not win a Club Show, but it will suit this project admirably.

The F1 generation will look like Normal Chinchillas, although probably rather dark - more like the Giganta. Mated together, they will produce nine Normals, three Chinrex and one Fox-Rex. You will obviously keep any Fox-Rex which turn up, and it would also be worth keeping the best-looking Chinrex, as two-thirds of these will carry the Tan-pattern gene. Obviously the task from then onwards will be to breed out the guard hairs which one must expect to find, at the same time retaining the ticking.

One word of warning: the Foxes may look very much like Otters in their baby coats - many Chinchillas and Chinrex are brown where they should be white practically until they become full adults. Rest, assured that it is impossible to breed a true Otter by this method, but it may take several generations of selective breeding before the brown tinge disappears.

The Fawn

"Saddle to be a bright golden fawn without any trace of creaminess, carried well down the flanks, gradually shading to a white belly. Colour to extend down the fur as far as possible, clearly defined white undercolour. Eye-circles, inside of ears, jowl and underside of tail to be white. Chest to match flanks. Head, outside of ears and forepaws to match saddle.

FAULTS: White hairs, blue sheen on coat, bluish or brownish tinge on points, bluish undercolour, very heavily barred front feet."

Of all the rex rabbits I have ever handled, only two had coats which are permanently etched in my memory. One was an Ermine which scooped the pool at one of the early London shows; the other was a Fawn – sadly, most fanciers had to be told what it was, such being the rarity of the breed at the time (the late 1960's).

Bred and shown throughout the country by my late friend George

Fawn exhibited by Mrs Pat Gaskin, Bradford Ch Show 2001

Denwood, this one rabbit can truly be said to have put the Fawn on the map. Whilst the variety had always had its devotees, the sheer quality of this rabbit did more to increase its popularity than any publicity could have hoped. From being the poor cousin of the Orange, in a few years the Fawn almost equalled them in numbers, and regularly beat them for the C.C., so much so that many societies, which just a few years previously would have been quite content to let them take their chance in A.O.V. class, were now forced to put on separate classes for each colour.

Regrettably the Fawn is now back in the hands of just the few. It still shares a specialist club with its close relative, the Orange, and in many cases it shares the same parents!

Although these two colours can be, and often are, bred together, it is doubtful if this practise is of long-term benefit to either breed. Whilst many Fawns still have excellent coats, and might improve this aspect of the Orange, they cannot really be expected to help with its colour. Whilst the colour of the Fawn should have a distinct golden shade, which might be improved with a "dash" of Orange, too much of this will lead to a distinct reddish tinge, which is not wanted. Whilst some breeders still keep both colours, most would agree that they are better if bred separately.

The exact colour required is rather difficult to put into words: golden without being reddish; too dark and it will carry a brownish tinge, too light and it will be creamy. The nearest approach I know is the colour of a "rich-tea" biscuit, and this shade should be level over as much of the back and sides as possible. Some shading is inevitable, and the standard allows for this. It will probably be found that, like the Orange, those with the least white undercolour carry the best tops – some Fawns I have seen had no undercolour at all, and looked none the worse for it!

Although the standard does not say so explicitly, there should be no trace of "mealiness" of flakiness to the colour. Although light in shade it must be solid, and again, a reduction in the width of the undercolour will help. A bluish sheen to the top colour is, unfortunately, only too easy to breed in, so that the rabbit looks more like a poor Lynx.

This fault is often associated with bluish undercolour and points; it is one of the few conditions which a mating with an Orange might remedy. The other faults – white hairs and very heavily barred feet, are not too often seen, and should not be tolerated in breeding stock.

Is it likely that the Fawn could make a comeback? It is tempting to speculate that it might not have needed to make one, had the Fawn specialists set up their own club during its heyday; since they were part of one of the liveliest set-ups in the fancy at that time, it is hardly surprising that they did not do so.

History has shown us that just one outstanding rabbit can re-create a demand; if that should happen again, or there were to be a general uplifting in numbers of all the rexes, then the Fawn breeders might well consider going it alone.

The Otter

"COLOUR:

BLACK: Body colour to be lustrous black, uniform throughout, with slate blue undercolour to reach the skin.

BLUE: A clear, bright, medium shade of blue (not lavender) throughout, from tip of fur to skin.

CHOCOLATE: A rich, dark chocolate with a purplish sheen, the colour to go well down the hairs with a pearly grey undercolour, eye colour brown.

LILAC: A pinky dove grey throughout from tip of fur to skin, bluish tinge a fault.

MARKINGS: The belly and undersides of the chin and tail to be creamy white with blue or white undercolour, to be divided from the body colour by a distinct border of tan. Nostrils and nape of neck to be tan. Eye circles and inside ears to be fawn. Chest to be a mixture of black and tan, merging with the main body colour: The fore feet on the front shall be predominantly black, the tan border between belly and flanks shall be continued down to the hind feet.

FAULTS: Brown or rusty tinge to the body colour. White or tan hairs other than in the patterned areas. Grey belly surface colour."

Officially, this breed was imported from the Continent, and standardised in 1976. Unofficially, they had been bred in this country

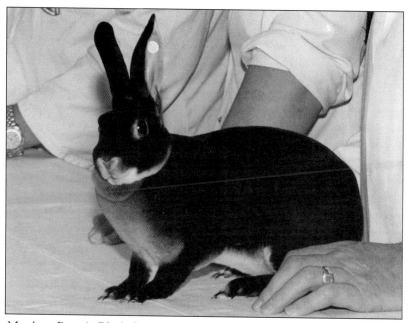

Matthew Preece's Black Otter, best Rex at the West Midlands Ch Show 2002

for many years before and after the war, in the process of producing Martens and Foxes; attempts to have them standardised were always rejected by the "powers-that-be" on the grounds that they were crossbreeds. It was, perhaps, hardly surprising that many of the old hands took grave exception to their acceptance as a standard variety; rex breeders on the whole are a placid lot, but this subject involved me, as secretary of one of the umbrella rex clubs at the time, in more controversy, and sometimes acrimonious correspondence, than any other matter before or since. All that is now history, and the pattern has become recognised, for good or ill, in other breeds apart from the rex.

Most of the credit for the eventual acceptance of the Otter must go to the late E J (Jock) Hardwicke of Billericay, and whatever might be thought of the merits of establishing the breed, one could not but admire the persistence Jock showed when the sudden imposition of quarantine regulations meant that all he had to start with was one young doe – not in kindle. This doe, and her descendants, must have been mated to nearly every other colour of rex, and to normal Tans, before Jock was satisfied. Others (myself included) had shown that they could easily be bred from Blacks crossed to Foxes or Martens, and would invariably be better coated and typed than the continental import; in all fairness, however, the "Tarka" stock tended to have much better colour. Once the variety became established, it achieved quite a degree of popularity and some notable wins, but the fundamental argument against the Otter as a separate variety remains, and always will.

The plain fact is that "Otter" as a genetically inherited colour or pattern, does not exist: the primary colour and pattern genes are exactly the same as those carried by the Tan. It is only the "modifying" genes which the Tan fanciers have so painstakingly bred into their stock over a century or so which has resulted in the rich tan all over the patterned areas; with the same eye to selective breeding, the same would be achieved in the rex, where we have, for years, had a standard but not rabbits! The creamy-white belly with tan border is really a half-way house, and to the purists this did not qualify the breed for recognition.

That being said, it is probably just as difficult to breed and maintain the belly colour to the correct standard as it would be to make it entirely tan (or white). At one time the bellies were well on the way to being tan all over, but now far too many have moved in the opposite direction, having just a muddy brown line between flanks and belly, which all too often has such a heavy blue undercolour that the overall effect is grey - most unattractive and definitely not to standard. This sort of Otter invariably fails on top colour, with the rest of the markings being a dull brown rather than tan and, equally invariably, has breeds other than the Otter in its immediate ancestry!

Another problem, which was at one time very prominent, can be an excess of tan hairs on the body and, most particularly, on the face. This fault seems to go hand-in-glove with an excess of tan on the belly, so attention to the one point will usually improve both. By far the worst colour fault, though, must be the blue or grey belly. Even the die-hard antagonists would always admit that the Otter, with its glistening top colour, contrasting with the white belly and tan border, had an attraction of its own; this is completely lost if the belly is not fully up to standard.

There was a time when some very presentable Chocolates could be seen, together with the odd Blue and Lilac. Unfortunately, this was before these colours were standardised, and since they became accepted they seem to have disappeared! This is a pity, as the Chocolate in particular is highly attractive, and so would the Lilac be if the correct light shade of top colour could be produced. The Blue would suffer from lack of intensity in the tanning, and is perhaps never going to gain any real popularity, but the other two colours could easily be produced by crossing to the Selfs. To be sure of permanent success, one ought to make sure that the Otter used had real intensity of tanning, since this would inevitably be degraded for a few generations in the outcross.

A good Otter is an attractive animal in its own right, and I would have no qualms about putting one up for B.I.S. if it was good enough.

The Marten Smoke Pearl

The same colour basically as the Siamese, but with white belly, eye circles, inside the ears, line of jaws, inside nostrils, inside of legs and feet, underside of tail and triangle behind the ears. The chest, flanks, rump and feet should be ticked with white hairs.

Since the belly colour in the Marten is white, it might be thought to be an easier proposition than the Siamese, as there are less shadings to worry about, and the pattern of the white markings generally takes care of itself.

One major problem, of course, is the ticking, which, if it were to protrude above the surface of the fur would be considered a fault. Those which I have seen in recent years have tended to be long in coat, possibly due to fairly recent Normal ancestry. With the great strides which have been made with the Siamese, there is no reason why the improvement in quality should not be transferred to the Marten. As the dominant pattern, it could soon out-number the Siamese.

The Tan

"Body colour to be either black, blue, lilac or chocolate, and to go down as far as possible. Belly, chest, eye circles, inside ears, underside of jowl and triangle to be rich tan. Face and outside ears to match body colour.

FAULTS: Rusty body colour, tan hairs on back and outside ears.

DISQUALIFICATIONS: White patches in armpits. (Saddle to extend from nape of neck to tail)."

The last proviso, regarding the saddle, has been repeated unchanged in every standards publication I have seen, going back to 1945 and probably further, but what does it mean? How can a Tan have a saddle? I suspect that many years ago this sentence must have been accidentally transposed from another standard, (possibly the Smoke Pearl) and has never been queried. Why not? For the simple reason that, as far as I can ascertain, no-one has yet succeeded in breeding a Tan-rex to show standard. I did make rather a half-hearted attempt thirty years ago, but domestic problems - and the standardisation of the Otter - put paid to that experiment at the F1 stage.

The breeders of the normal Tan took decades to change their belly colour from cream to the rich tan we see today; we could, with luck, do the job much more quickly today with the rex, and what a beautiful animal that would be. However, the breeding of new colours into any variety inevitably takes time; the experimenters naturally like to get their stock out for people to see, knowing that there is still a great deal of work to be done on it, and most judges will make allowances in the early years. We have seen this happen with the Mini-rex, but what would happen if someone did try to produce a genuine Tan? Unless it were well-nigh perfect in colour it would automatically be regarded as a too "hot" Otter and thrown off the table!

I would really like to think that there is someone out there looking for a real challenge; someone who has the space and the patience to labour away out of the spotlight, knowing that the chances of having anything worth showing are at least five years away, probably longer.

My advice is that I would take advantage of the existence now of the Otter, and use it. Mind you, the foundation stock would have to be pretty special, in that you are going to need maximum size, very good top colour and coat, and belly colour without any trace of blue to it.

It would really need to be much more orange on the belly than is ideal on the Otter, but in other respects it must be so close to the standard that you would need to practice your half-nelsons to get the owner to part with it! I was once wagered by Jock Hardwicke that with such an animal he could produce the Tan inside three generations; as far as I know he never tried it, because three generations is much too optimistic. There would have to be absolutely no doubt in anyone's mind that the rabbit was a Tan and not an Otter, and for that a little outside assistance is going to be needed.

This can only be obtained by using the normal Tan, with all its attendant disadvantages. You are bound to introduce poor coats, guard hairs and small size, but you must find from somewhere that richness of coloration, and there is no other logical source. What is needed is something which, to the Tan fancier, is too big and carries too much tan, and this might easily be available.

You will, by the time the outcross is needed, have been selectively breeding your Otters for extension of the tanning onto the belly for two or three generations (at the same time maintaining type, size, top colour and coat). Any further improvement to the belly colour is going to be very slow in coming, but this 'line' must be kept going.

At the same time you must start another line by mating one or two does to the sort of Tan I have described. This will produce youngsters with normal coats, half-way between the Rex and the Tan for size and type, but with better belly colour than the rex you used. These youngsters should be bred together until you have enough rex to work with: as only twenty-five percent can be expected, you may well need plenty of litters! These rex must now be selectively bred with the primary aim of establishing a true tanned belly. Apart from the obvious considerations of health and fecundity, the other parameters are of secondary importance.

It will take several generations before you are consistently breeding stock with the correct colour, but lacking in size and coat compared with the Otters you are still breeding from line one. Now is the time to start a third line by crossing the two existing ones: sit back and keep your fingers firmly crossed!

One of two things will happen. With great good luck you will find your progeny will have the size and coats of the Otters, with the belly colour from the Tan line, and your task may appear complete. You will have so succeeded in "fixing" the desirable points in the first two lines that you only have dominant genes, and your improved stock, obtained by combining the two lines, are technically F1 hybrids.

This is a technique much employed by commercial animal and plant breeders to establish reliable colour, size and growth characteristics to such an extent that suppliers of seeds and day-old chicks can virtually offer a guarantee of performance. You would be able to do the same with your Tan-rexes. Every one born would be a potential champion, but - be warned - like the commercial products, they will not breed true. All the recessive genes in one line have been masked by dominant ones from the other, but will surely come back to haunt you!

If you should find yourself in this apparently fortunate situation, you must keep your original lines going, as the hybrids will only be fit for show!

That situation, it must be admitted, is highly Utopian. It would have happened in any breed, at any time, had the necessary facilities and incentives existed. It requires a great degree of inbreeding, and the setting up of, not one line of each type but several, to guard against any inbreeding to extinction, which is a distinct possibility.

The most likely thing to happen is that your two original lines will not have been that closely inbred, and consequently there will be a considerable variation in the progeny. You should, however, now be able to select stock which, whilst slightly deficient in some aspects, excels in others – in other words you can revert to the normal pattern of selective breeding with which we are all familiar.

Conversely, you might find that the progeny combine all the bad points of their parents. Never mind, they wouldn't breed true either, what you have put in must come out, so breed them together until it does.

A very lengthy dissertation indeed on an extinct variety, but the principles are applicable to many experiments. I do hope it may create an awakening interest in what, on paper, could be the exhibition rex par excellence.

THE AGOUTI BREEDS

The Castor

"**Colour to be dark rich chestnut brown. Intermediate colour to be rich orange clearly defined in a dark slate blue undercolour. Orange and dark slate blue to be equal (half and half). Fur to be lightly tipped with black, chest to match flanks. Head, outside of ears, upperside of tail to match body colour, ears laced black. Belly and underside of tail white with dark slate blue undercolour.**

FAULTS: Heavy black top, greyness on haunches. Barred front feet."

Here we have the original colour of rex; the progenitor of all that have followed since those first mutations; in the eyes of many, the most attractive shade of all. By all that is logical, it should also be the most numerous, and yet it never has been. Possibly the earliest specimens were not so attractive a colour as those which were subsequently bred. Certainly, the original imports suffered from a number of physical faults which could only be eradicated by outcrossing to other, more healthy, normal fur breeds; the new colours of rex thus produced would have had a great novelty value whereas the Castors in the same litters would have lost a great deal of their richness in colour. If one thing is certain about the Castor, it is that it does not take kindly to an outcross.

Whatever the reason may have been for the failure of the Castor to scale the heights in terms of numbers, it has always had its devoted followers, possibly more so

Castor doe exhibited by Mr & Mrs J H Phillips at Bradford Ch Show 2001

than any other breed. It is a proven fact that, once a fancier is smitten by the Castor, it will exert a lifelong fascination; many, many people have sampled the breed, probably found it not so easy to breed to standard as they thought, and gone on to another variety, or even out of rabbits altogether. Nine times out of ten they are back in a few years, wondering how on earth they could ever have contemplated giving up this infuriatingly difficult, but compellingly addictive rabbit!

How best to put into words the elusive colour of the Castor? The standard does its best – it could, I suppose, have compared it with the Belgian Hare which it very closely resembles. The most apt description I have ever come across compared it with the colour of a newly-ripened Horse Chestnut, and if you aim for this shade you will not go far wrong.

Like all coats which have a lot of yellow pigment, the colour of the Castor can only really be properly assessed in natural daylight; so many show halls, with their fluorescent or even sodium lighting, do not do the Castor and its kin justice. If you are judging or considering buying one in such a venue, take the rabbit outside before deciding if it is a good colour or not.

The chief contributory factor to the overall colour is the band of orange – ideally this should be even deeper and richer than that on the Orange rex, and many of the best ones are. A lemon yellow is all-too-often seen, giving the rabbit a wild-grey appearance, whilst at the other extreme a dull brick-red is to be avoided; it must be said that there are not too many rabbits seen with this fault now, they tended to go with very heavy tops, resulting in a very dark, almost purplish overall effect. Not only must the orange band be deep and rich, it must also be even throughout its length - no tendency to be good at the top and paler towards the base. It should also be approximately half the length of the hair shaft, and it is a very rare specimen which does not diverge from this ideal on some parts of the pelt.

To many breeders, it is the top colour which makes or mars the Castor, and converts what would be a flat orange into that glowing chestnut. Too little ticking and the top will be dull and lifeless; too much and it will be spoiled. The ideal top will have alternate guard hairs very lightly tipped, so giving an equal mixture of black and orange.

In far too many cases, every hair is tipped, and this extends too far down the hair shaft, a common fault in all Agoutis today.

The base colour, of dark slate blue, cannot be seen until the fur is parted, but is of equal importance to the other colour aspects. It must be dark without being grey or black, it must not tend to get paler towards the skin, and it must extend over the belly.

Quite a common fault is for the slate to be rather pale, slightly less than half the length of the coat, and not carried through onto the belly. Very often with such a specimen, the top colour is lighter and to some eyes at least as attractive as the standard says, but this is an insidious fault; the next generation will have even narrower and paler slate, and the next one none at all, and no ticking either.

Whilst the slate may, in some people's eyes, be little more than a "fancy" point, it is, if you will pardon the pun, absolutely basic to the make-up of a good Castor. I am not saying that one should not breed from a rabbit which is less than perfect in the slate – it may well have other important attributes – but its partner must excel in that department.

The "definition", the clear dividing line between slate and orange, is again often regarded by the novice as a "fancy" point, but is, in fact, the hallmark of a well-bred Castor. Naturally, the definition cannot be fully clear if the rabbit is in a moult; in fact the Castor probably shows the moult more than any other rex, which may be another factor which has held it back. Nevertheless, a clear division is desired and achievable; show me a Castor with poor definition and I'll find something other than Castor in its recent ancestry!

By the very nature of the agouti patterning, the Castor will tend to be several shades lighter on the flanks and chest than the rest of the body, but it has been proved that they can be bred to be more or less level all over, and they look all the better for it. Even the best of specimens tend to be a shade paler on the haunches, but fortunately the old bogey of grey haunches has almost disappeared. This is almost certainly due to the improvement in the richness of the orange band, which may also have contributed to the reduction in barring of the front feet.

This is still a contentious issue in some quarters; until comparatively recently it was a fault in all rex, and I'm sure the majority of Castor breeders, whilst recognising that it is so endemic in agoutis as to be regarded as almost part of the pattern, realise it is part of the challenge to breed it out. It can be done, and just adds that finishing touch.

Ears should be laced black, i.e. black line round the outer edges, with black ticking on the fronts. Many an otherwise good-looking specimen can be found with wild-grey colouring to the ears, although it will generally be found that these are also somewhat deficient in the orange band.

There was much debate in years gone by as to whether the slate and orange should be half and half (or 50/50 as most old hands still call it). At first sight it might appear that, so long as the shade of orange was correct, it did not much matter whether it occupied half the fur length or a quarter, in fact the old standards allowed for a 75%/25% split between slate and orange. There was probably a coupled tendency towards dark tops with these proportions, but more importantly it did not sufficiently discourage those specimens with only 20% or less orange; only a minor divergence from the standard, but invariably cross-breds. We are better able to deal with these now!

Although relatively few in numbers, the majority of Castors seen today approach very close to the standard in colour, a great improvement on the brown-greys which were once prevalent.

How do they fare for type and coat? One of the most famous strains of Castors was the "Riverside" of the 1940's and 50's, renowned for type and heads on the bucks like Hereford bulls. We don't often see bucks like that now, but at least, in general, they are obviously masculine, and one could not say that type is a particular problem, although some do tend to be long in body.

Coats, however, are a different proposition. I have a theory that, the more protein the rabbit needs to manufacture pigment, the less it will have available for its coat. That may be far too simplistic a view, but it is a fact that even the best Castors ever seen would not have beaten the Ermines, Seals and Blacks on density. There are hopeful signs that matters are improving here, whilst the very long coats seem to be a thing of the past.

Quite the biggest problem appears to be one which was thought to have been bred out forty years ago, but now seems to affect nearly every strain, namely the production of recessives. In the early days, the Castor was used to produce just about every other colour, and just about every colour would naturally turn up in their litters. Twenty years or more of selective breeding was supposed to have eliminated the "odd" colours, but today the problem seems to have intensified.

This can only be put down to misguided attempts to "improve" the Castor with other colours; whether this has had any effect on coat or colour which could not have been achieved by selective breeding within the variety is debatable.

What cannot be denied is that far too many Castors are liable to breed litters containing just about everything EXCEPT Castors. I know of one or two converts who have been completely disenchanted when this happened to them; to breed a Castor anywhere near the standard is difficult enough, but when you only get one or two to choose from in every litter it gets more than a little frustrating.

If the Castors which are actually produced are good ones, you can console yourself in the knowledge that you strike a higher average than, say, the Dutch fancier, and that if you consistently breed only Castor/Castor the recessives will disappear eventually.

If, on the other hand, you are only breeding the occasional Castor and it is rubbish, you have been the victim of indiscriminate cross-breeding, and there may be no true Castors in the make-up of your stock. The only solution here is to go to a reputable breeder and start again. Rex breeders in general are a happy, friendly bunch, always willing to help at little cost.

Chinrex

"Fur to be lightly tipped with black and white, giving a sparkling chinchillated effect. Intermediate colour to be near white clearly defined on a dark slate blue undercolour, with a minimum of one third and a maximum of one half near white. Chest to match flanks. Head, outside ears and upperside of tail to be chinchillated grey. Ears lacked black. Eye circles, inside ears and underside jowl pearl grey. Belly

and underside of tail white.
FAULTS: Rusty tinge, heavy black top."

"Nature's masterpiece in fur" was the description dreamed up for the Chinrex many years ago, and very apt it is; it is the nearest approach in any domesticated animal to the wild Chinchilla Lanigera of the Andes. One of the first rexes to be produced after the Castor, it was the colour in greatest demand by the fur trade, and many highly fashionable garments were produced, even for royalty.

Thanks to the very publicity-conscious specialist club, the Chinrex achieved a very high popularity rating in the 1960's and 70's; entries of over fifty were expected at their stock shows, and even a monthly points class (which were held all over the country) would usually attract two dozen rabbits. Whether the overall quality matched the quantity is open to question; what was very noticeable was that, with a points class every month, breeders tended to ignore the other shows, with the result that they were soon relegated to the A.O.V., and very few people ever saw one. Today, the breed adopts a much lower profile, and is none the worse for it. In common with most rex, numbers are well down from their peak, but I would say that the average quality is much higher now, with a high proportion of the winners doing well in the duplicate classes.

This is one of the few standards which is almost self-explanatory - to all intents and purposes one can visualise the animal from the written word. One or two aspects do, however, require a little comment and elaboration, firstly the top colour.

Although the fur should be tipped with black AND white, most are not; the norm is for every

The "Ideal Chinrex". From a colour plate by Wippell published in *Fur & Feather* in 1930

hair to be tipped with black, to a greater or lesser extent. At best, this results in a rather dull, flat top; at worst, in a very heavy black one. The occasional specimen is seen which does have white ticking as well, but in many cases this comprises guard hairs which just protrude, and spoil the levelness of both coat and colour. A reduction in length of these guard hairs would give us the really sparkling effect. Even a slightly heavy top will prevent the near-white, or "pearling" from showing through whilst the animal is not moving, which removes much of the beauty of the breed.

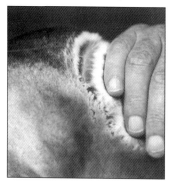

"Near-white" is taken by most breeders as meaning as close to white as possible – the greater the contrast between base, intermediate band and tipping, the better the overall effect. The Chinrex breeders have considerably more latitude in terms of the width of the intermediate band than do the Castor fanciers, and in theory a band of as little as one quarter would only be a minor fault.

Speaking on behalf of the many judges who have been confronted with an animal of this sort, might I suggest it should be a major fault, if not a disqualification. It is very easy indeed to produce a Chinrex with very narrow pearling, possibly a slightly dark top, but with such size, and wealth of coat as to put in straight to the top of the class. You produce them by cross-breeding to Martens or Foxes, and do the breed no service at all.

As with all agoutis, chest and flanks will be a little lighter than the saddle, but should not be very noticeably so. No mention is made of the undercolour on the belly: if the animal has a sound slate base then you will generally find that the undercolour on the belly is also slate, but, of course, it should only be visible when the fur is parted.

Sometimes we see a top which, whilst not exactly rusty, has a rather purplish tinge; this generally indicates that the animal is about to break into a moult. This will be the case if the skin has turned blue; if not, then that breeder has got real problems!

So far, I have made no mention of barred front feet because, rightly or wrongly, the standard no longer mentions them either - the only one for an agouti not to do so. Sooner or later, if the barring is allowed to get out of hand, the white streaks will lose their slate base and extend right to the skin, and thus become a white patch.

The Cinnamon

"Colour to be bright golden tan. Intermediate colour to be light orange clearly defined on a blue undercolour. Fur lightly tipped with brown. Chest to match flanks. Head, outside ears, upperside of tail to match body colour. Ears laced brown. Belly and underside of tail white with blue undercolour. Blue and orange bands to be approximately equal in width.

FAULTS: Fawny tinge, dark blotches, barred front feet."

This must be considered a breed for a connoisseur: at its best it resembles an Orange with the top colour enriched by the very light dusting of brown ticking; at worst, it looks like a muddy, washed-out Castor. I think it is true to say that there has never been a stud dedicated to the Cinnamon, the vast majority having been bred from Castors.

Very many of the old Castor breeders valued stock which turned up Cinnamons, as they reckoned that this line of breeding produced the best coloured Castors. Whilst this has never been proved conclusively, my own experience leads me to believe that the 'brown' gene, even when carried as a recessive, does have the effect of intensifying and brightening the orange pigment. Many of the best coloured Oranges have been proved to derive from the Cinnamon rather than the Castor - when crossed with a Havana, the F1's are Cinnamons and not Castors.

That would be one way of founding a strain of Cinnamons if one were lucky enough to find an Orange carrying the brown genes. There would, however, be one major disadvantage, in that the Orange would inevitably introduce a paleness to the undercolour which would be extremely difficult to eliminate.

A more certain method would be to cross the Havana with a Castor; don't expect any Cinnamons until the F2 generation, where they should appear in the proportion of three in sixteen. This is obviously a rather slow procedure, but should give a sound slate

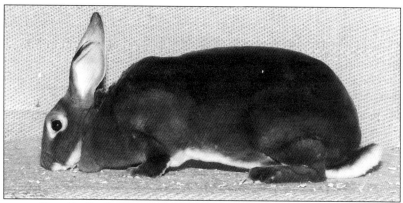

Caneddy Stud's Cinnamon, exhibited at Bradford Ch Show 2000

base on which to build the rest of the colour.

There will obviously be a high proportion of Castors in the F2 litters, often of such a poor colour that you might think they were Cinnamons, particularly in the baby coat. The ear lacings will always tell you the truth – no matter how indistinct the rest of the colour, a Cinnamon will always have brown ear lacing.

So few Cinnamons have been shown in recent years that it is impossible to generalise on faults. Some I have seen were very much lacking in type and size, but that is not at all likely to be a problem if one were to start from scratch, with animals well up to standard in that respect.

I don't think I am alone in having more than a sneaking regard for the Cinnamon, and a few generations of selective breeding could well result in a real eye-opener.

The Lynx

"Colour to be orange-shot-silver. Intermediate colour to be bright orange clearly defined on white undercolour. Tips of fur silver. Belly, eye circles, inside ears and underside of jowl white. Chest to match flanks. Serious faults: bluish tinge on top; blue undercolour; barred front feet."

With the Lynx, we have what must be regarded as the saddest 'decline and fall' story in the entire history of the Rex. I may well be indulging in hindsight with the benefit of rose-tinted spectacles, but one of my earliest recollection is of a class of Lynx in about 1950, or possibly earlier. A late winter sun was shining on the pens, and the rabbits outdid the sunset! They exhibited a really deep orange glow, overlaid with a subtle silvery sheen. I was utterly captivated, but was never able to obtain stock, the prices they then commanded being beyond the pocket of an impecunious school-boy.

What has gone wrong, and why? As to the first part of the question - just about everything! Too little stock and too few breeders, all with virtually the same strain.

Inbreeding has led to conformation faults, difficulty in getting does in kindle and small litter sizes. The only Lynx I ever had just would not mate, whatever ruses were tried.

Of the few which are bred each year, most are faulty in type, lacking in density and have much too heavy ticking on top – rather than being very lightly tipped with silver, practically every hair has a dull grey band extending nearly a quarter of the way down the hair shaft. This completely masks the orange, resulting in an unattractive, almost muddy overall effect.

I have said before that most Agoutis are far too heavy on top-colour, and it applies with double force to the Lynx. I think it highly probable that the majority of rex fanciers today have never seen a good coloured Lynx, and this includes a lot of the current breeders. The standard is quite explicit, the colour should be orange, shot with silver - we are suffering from "over-kill"! Until the correct balance can be restored, the breed will never make any progress.

Why this state of affairs has come about is probably due to a combination of factors, rather than one major disaster. At one time it was permissible for the orange band to merge gradually with the white undercolour; the change in the standard to call for clear definition must have eliminated several strains.

At the same time some of the leading judges felt that the orange band was taking on too reddish a hue: several breeders must have felt that they were then being penalised for their success. Whilst a brick-red colour might not be exactly to standard, it was felt by many to be infinitely preferable to the pale, lemony shade which some were putting up in preference.

The result: the loss of more erstwhile breeders, and a lack of recruitment of newcomers. No novice will be tempted to take up a breed in which even the experts disagree on their aims.

When the Lynx was in its heyday, a list of their most successful breeders was more like a roll-call of the great and good in the rex fancy: it is very clear that they did not pass on enough good stock to follow on when they themselves had gone.

On a brighter note, there has always been a nucleus of stock with a good white base colour, clear definition and reasonably rich and level orange band; only the very heavy top colour prevents it from being seen!

I did once see a Lynx Satin which literally had everything - until you reached the undercolour, which was a real slate-blue! Nevertheless, if I had been a Lynx breeder and been offered that rabbit, I'd have been on my way home with it before the owner had a chance to change his mind!

On basic theory, at least, the Lynx could be recreated by crossing a Cinnamon with an Opal – it is, after all, a Lilac Agouti. Apart from the obvious fact that there are even fewer of those colours in existence now than there are Lynx, the major problem is that all the other agoutis require a slate blue undercolour.

Whilst the diluting genes would lighten this to some extent, it would still be blue and not white (as was that Satin). The white is brought about by modifying genes, the same ones which account

J J Webb's Lynx, Bradford Ch Show 1999

for the "snow-balls" in Blues and Lilacs; many an Opal has been ruined by these genes, and a white-undercoloured Opal would have to be my first choice for an outcross - in the unlikely event that one were to be available.

As far as the other Agoutis are concerned, only the Orange or Fawn would be remotely suitable; I've seen some pretty disastrous results from their being introduced into the Castor, but they might-just might-lighten the top colour without too great an effect on the undercolour and orange band.

The only other colour I would seriously consider would be the Lilac, and then only if it was a "snow-ball". Like the Lynx, the Lilac has its problems with inbred degeneration, and crossing the two might be of mutual benefit, although I would guess that the Lynx would gain more than the Lilac would. The resultant F1's should certainly be much more viable than either of their parents. Hopefully, the undercolour will be practically white, but the orange band is very likely to be narrow and pale, with no improvement as yet in the top colour.

It therefore follows that the Lynx used must be the very best available, and the most promising youngsters mated back to it. At the same time, they could be mated inter se; this would be a rather slower way of getting back to an exhibition-type Lynx, but it would also produce a proportion of Lilacs which could be bred back into that variety.

I know that the Lynx breeders - few as they are - are only too aware of all the problems I have been discussing, and will not be offended by my doing so. If not, I hope some of my suggestions might bear fruit. The Lynx once held a coveted position in the rex world. That it slipped from its pedestal is no fault of anyone connected with the breed today; a little enterprise and a lot of dedication might well put it back within the next decade.

The Opal

"Top colour pale shade of blue with a layer of golden tan between it and the slate blue undercolour. General effect to be blue-shot tan. Belly, eye circles, inside ears and underside of jowl white. Slate and orange bands to be approximately equal in width, belly to be white with blue

undercolour.
FAULTS: barred front feet."

A very appealing mixture of blue and gold, most rex fanciers cannot understand why it has never gained any popularity (those of us who have tried breeding them could easily explain the reason!).

My late guide and mentor, Chas Dickens, was the only person I know who ever bred them seriously, but despite all his efforts in supplying stock to all parts of the country, when he died, the breed died with him; such stock as he had left was beyond breeding, although several of us tried. The late Bill Bates and I then got together and created the breed again from scratch, with some success, and some of this stock is still in existence, so all hope is not lost!

The biggest difficulty with the Opal is in obtaining the correct slate blue undercolour without getting too dark a top. It is relatively easy to get a light blue top, but very difficult indeed to get this without the undercolour becoming white. The cause of this is obviously the gene or genes which result in the "snow-balls" in the Blue, and once established the only answer is an outcross – preferably to a Castor. This is obviously the breed to use if creating a strain from scratch, mated to a Blue.

Here, however, we must be careful not to use a "snow-ball", and preferably one with no "snow-balls" in its ancestry – if such a thing exists. Even the best strains of Opals - Chas's not excepted - have always produced a proportion of youngsters with white undercolour: often this will become darker with age, and such stock generally has a nice pale top colour.

You could expect to win a few C.C.s with a rabbit like this, but don't BREED from one. Good breeding stock will have a slate undercolour as soon as it begins to show; concentrate on fixing this characteristic into a strain, and confining the tipping to the very end of the hair shaft.

Many good Opals have been unfairly penalised by judges on the grounds that the slate is not deep enough a shade, and the tan not rich enough – they seem to want a Castor with a blue top! This is a genetic impossibility, and not what the standard calls for.

The dilution gene does exactly that – the slate blue is usually the shade seen on the blue Dutch, and provided that it is the same shade

Opal bred by Ron Willers

down to the skin, is perfectly in accordance with the standard. Likewise with the tan or orange band; the natural tendency with the dilute gene is for orange to be converted to fawn.

Provided that the Castor used to found the strain had a rich orange band, then the fawn shade, by selective breeding, will become a golden tan as called for, but it will never be as deep and rich as the colour seen in the Castor, or even the Lynx. Please note there is no mention in the standard of DARK slate blue, or RICH orange.

The top colour of the Opal could, in theory, extend further down the hair shaft than it does on the Lynx: note that the former requires to be "blue-shot-tan" whilst the Lynx should be "orange-shot-silver", so that the first impression of the Opal should be of a blue rabbit, with a touch of tan which will become more pronounced as the rabbit moves.

Nevertheless, I would always aim for as little tipping as possible; if the slate base is to be maintained, then there will always be a tendency for the shade of the top colour to be just a little darker than ideal, so the less there is of it, the better.

The standard for the belly colour was changed some years ago from "white" to "white with blue under". Can you imagine the difficulties the pioneers had in getting a pure white colour on the belly without sacrificing the slate blue on the rest of the body? This was a case of changing the standard, not to suit the rabbits being bred, but for the betterment of the breed.

Strangely enough, the dilute gene does not seem to result in such a tendency for the coat to curl as it does in the Blue and Lilac; in fact most of the Opals seen on the show-bench have quite dense coats, although, as with most agoutis, the length has to be kept under close control. Type has never been a problem, no doubt due to the influence of the Castors in the very near ancestry.

There are other ways of producing Opals apart from the Castor/ Blue method: a Fawn crossed with a Blue would produce Opals of a sort even in the F1 generation, as it would if mated to a Smoke Pearl or even a blue Otter. In none of these instances, however, is there any background of slate undercolour or definition. This can only come from the Castor or, at a pinch, the Cinnamon.

In my opinion, the only safe way is a good coloured Castor to a "non-snowball" Blue. An F1 generation of "Brown-grey" type Castors will then produce Castors, Opals, Blacks and Blues in the standard ratio 9:3:3:1.

I would have to hazard a guess, though, that even when a strain of Opals is produced, the occasional cross back to the Castor is going to be beneficial, if not essential. Good specimens of both colours have been bred in the same litter, but this is hardly the way to establish a good strain of either breed.

OTHER VARIETIES

This section includes those with patterns which do not fit into any of the previous categories; those derived from other breeds and for which no separate standards have ever been produced; Satins; the rough coated varieties, and the latest introduction, the Mini-Rex. For reasons which may become obvious, I will leave till the very last that paragraph which begins "Harlequin (Japanese), English, Dutch, etc., and begin with the Dalmatian (pictured on previous page).

The Dalmatian
"Coat is non-pigmented, that is to say white all over. The pattern consists of numerous little coloured patches covering the body, head and ears.
BICOLOUR: White body with pattern of one colour only.
TRICOLOUR: White body with pattern of two colours (i.e. black patches and fawn patches).
The patches can only be: black, blue, brown, orange or fawn. The colour to be carried down as far as possible. Eyes

Dalmatian Tri Colour exhibited by Goyfield Stud at Bradford Ch Show 1979

and ears to match appropriate colours, solid ears, eye circles and smut are allowable.

FAULTS: Not enough coloured patches.

DISQUALIFICATIONS: Pattern too much like that of a Butterfly or an English, i.e. with a resemblance of a saddle."

When this breed was first imported, the standard was criticised in some quarters as having somewhat suffered in translation. However, I'm sure we all know basically what is wanted – a white rabbit with spots on!

Originally, the Dalmatian was a much bigger rabbit than the English Rexes, and needed a bigger ring. Their coats were also long, coarse and completely lacking in density.

The Dalmatian of today has to meet the same standard for type and size as any other rex, and in general does so well, having size and shape without breaking the scales. Coats have, in many cases, come close to the standards of the more established colours, although there are still occasional throw-backs to the early "hearth-rugs". Generally speaking, the white in the coat is a pure colour – better than many Ermines – but there is a great deal of variation in the pattern.

The patterning is caused, of course, by the same genes which produce the English, and thus some will have few spots (and breed true), some will be self-coloured (and also breed true), whilst about half will be spotted more or less all over the body and will not breed true.

Since the standard requires numerous patches, these are obviously the ones to concentrate on, but certain features have to be carefully watched. The most obvious is that, since only fifty percent are likely to conform to standard anyway, large litter sizes are a must.

Secondly, too much marking on the back can easily lead to a pronounced saddle. Last, but by no means least, the more patches there are, the greater the tendency for them to merge into each other and become ugly blotches. Numerous AND small is the criterion, and sets the breeder of Dalmatians a problem many of us would not have the patience to tackle – this really is a Fancy rabbit with a rex coat.

Unlike the English, there is no set pattern of spotting to breed to, provided that there is no saddle. To me, therefore, it would seem entirely logical that, at least occasionally, a mating of lightly spotted "Charlie" to a Self bred from Dalmatians could be advantageous, if only because all the progeny would be patterned all over, giving a considerably wider choice for future breeding.

To breed the very lightly spotted ones together might eventually lead to an increase in the number of spots, without the tendency towards blotching. This is a course a lot of breeders must have tried, to judge by the number seen with the small half-moustache instead of the full butterfly smut.

To mate the "Charlie" to a properly patterned rabbit might be thought to lead to an increase in the numbers of patterned progeny – it won't! The self will be eliminated, but only to be replaced by an equivalent number of Charlies.

Another point I ought to mention is that there is a possibility of a lethal gene being coupled with the 'butterfly' gene; the English breeders, of course, would normally not bother to try to rear the "Charlie", but many who did try in the past reported great difficulty in getting them to thrive.

If a tricolour could be produced which was evenly spotted all over the body, it would look like a leopard – what an eye-catcher that would be! Whether that ideal is really feasible, I rather doubt. The natural tendency with the butterfly pattern is for the bulk of the coloured parts to be concentrated on the hinder portions of the body: the more the markings are broken up here, the greater will be the tendency for the rest of the body to be devoid of colour.

There is a great dilemma here: if the rabbit does not have SMALL patches, and they are not numerous, then it does not conform to standard: if they are small but too few in number, then it is a fault. Some clarification of the standard here would be of value to breeder and judge alike.

However we define the pattern, the patches must be of a good colour. The solid black and rich orange of a good tricolour is a striking contrast: here the latest standard must definitely be at fault – fawn patches go with blue, not black. Again, we have no guidance on shades in the other colours: should the blue be lavender or deep slate; should the brown be chocolate, or could it be agouti?

To many eyes, the Black/Orange tricolour; the first to be imported, is still the most attractive and the most interesting to breed, if only for the fact that the "selfs" produced show the harlequin pattern. Much to the chagrin of the people who have been trying to breed Harlequins for years, these very often carry as good a pattern as any normal, with a good rex coat to boot!

Great strikes have certainly been made with the Dalmatian in the past decade, and a good number can now compete on even terms with the other breeds as far as type and coat is concerned. Breeders must now concentrate on reducing the size of the patches, whilst increasing their number: easy to say, but a life-time's work for somebody!

Himalayan

"**Colour and Markings: Points to be dark seal. Body colour pure white. Nose markings to go well-up between eyes, into whisker beds and to be large and egg shaped. Ears, dense colour to roots. Front feet markings well up legs and down to toes. Hind foot markings well up hocks and down to toes, and tail dense to root.**

FAULTS: Creamy or yellow tinge in body colour, eye stains.

OTHER COLOUR POINTS RECOGNISED - Blue or chocolate.

COLOUR NOT RECOGNISED - Marten type points in all colours.**"

Here, at last, we have a success story. These chapters have been littered with examples of varieties which have never achieved the popularity they deserved, and with those which, whilst once popular, are at present so rare as to be on the verge of extinction. The Himalayan once came into the latter category; there was a period after the War when the Himalayan was just about the most frequently shown of all the rexes, but within ten short years it was, to all intents and purposes, extinct.

Since this is such a striking rabbit, and had been bred to a very high standard, it can hardly have been lack of interest which caused its demise. What is very obvious, though, is the pre-eminence attained

Himalayan Rex. Breeder unknown

by one exhibitor, J E Huddart of the 'Tintern Stud'. At its peak, his stock was unbeatable, and I would guess that, to remain in any way competitive, every breeder had to go to 'Tintern' for stock.

Thus, when inbred weaknesses began to become apparent, and Mr Huddart had died, there was no other strain to go to, and no suitable outcross.

From time to time, attempts were made to re-introduce the variety via the Californian, with the inevitable problems of too much bulk and not enough colour. It may well be that some of today's stock have that ancestry, whilst others are believed to have been chance-bred from Sables (which would not be an impossibility).

Whatever their source, it is very pleasing to be able to say that there are now sufficient Hims, and keen breeders, to have enabled the specialist club to be revived and, what is more to the point, the stock is GOOD. Nothing succeeds like success, and enough Best Rex awards were won by Himalayans in the 1990's to ensure a steady demand for stock; the more hands a variety is in, the less chance there will be of it dying out again.

I said the stock was good – just how good? Type and size, in general, well up to standard – no suspicion of the Normal Himalayan in their make-up! Coats, at least on the best ones, very good indeed, well able to compete with the best of the other colours; the occasional long-coated one is seen, which may be due to the Californian influence, but the fault is no more prevalent than in any other variety.

Body colour is, almost without exception, as pure as any Ermine (and purer than many). It is only on the question of the points that there is any amount of work still to be done.

The standard for the Normal Himalayan calls for the points to be black – yet after all the years they have been bred even the best are really only a dark sepia. The rex standard only calls for a seal colour, which must be interpreted as sepia, but there is no reason why they should not be bred to the same shade as the Normals, and as yet this has not been achieved.

Even the best have a suspicion of chocolate brown about them, particularly towards the ends of the leg markings. In general, there is no complaint about the extent of the markings here, just the colour. With regard to the nose markings, though, not very many could really be described as large and egg-shaped; they need to go further up between the eyes and into the whisker-beds. Bearing in mind how short a time it has been since the breed was re-introduced, this is a very small criticism indeed.

Eye stains are listed as a fault, and are, unfortunately, endemic to the pattern, generally being more prominent in colder weather. Whilst no specific mention is made of body stain, it is considered a very serious fault in the Normal; in the rex it has to count as a divergence from the pure white body colour called for, and be penalised accordingly. Therein lies a warning - if your Him has a piece of fur pulled out in winter, it will almost certainly grow back as a coloured patch.

The novice should be aware of one characteristic which has given many a breeder of the Normals nightmares when they have not been fully briefed. Open up a nest of young Hims - and you won't see any! Some will look like albinos, and others will be a slate blue colour all over. Never fear, by the time the intermediate coat grows they will be the proper colour; some contend that the ones which are slate in the nest grow up to have the best colour, but this has never been proved to be an invariable rule.

The standard caters for chocolate and blue points. I would venture the suggestion that it might be better to concentrate on the sepia points for a while longer and get them really well established. At the moment, the Himalayan is an oasis in the wilderness of the A.O.V. rexes – let's not allow it to become yet another mirage.

Silver Seal

"COLOUR: Jet black, silvering to be evenly distributed over the whole of the body, giving a sparkling effect, including ears, tail, feet and chest. Undercolour dark blue to skin."

To the best of my knowledge none of this variety have been shown in the pasty forty years, there are no photographs in existence and even before then there were no more than the odd one or two breeders at any time. Obviously derived from the Silver Grey - and apparently needing frequent back-crossing to that breed to maintain the silvering – the chances of the Silver Seal ever carrying a proper rex coat are slim indeed.

Not only that, but, for the silvering to be really noticeable, the coat would have to carry guard hairs which were considerably more pronounced than would be generally acceptable. I have to confess to having bred several of what might turn out to be Silver Seals, purely by accident; at certain stages of their development it seemed that they would become silvered over the whole body, but then they began to lose it in the next coat! On the ones which had anything like a proper rex coat, the silvering could only be seen when the fur was parted; only an excess of guard hairs made the silvering at all prominent.

It might well be that a better route to establishing the variety would be via the Argente de Champagne – at least that would result in denser, if longer coats than the Silver Grey could ever produce. However, there are several breeds which rely on guard hairs for their effect, and thus could not realistically be rexed, and I'm afraid this is one of them.

Satin Rex

"COAT - SMOOTH COATED: To be approximately half an inch in length, with fine Satin-like texture and sheen,

very dense and free from projecting guard hairs.
**ROUGH COATED: Coat to carry a curl or wave, even
over the whole body. The fur on ears, feet and tail may be
straight. Points: 50.**
**COLOUR AND/OR PATTERN: Any colour or pattern
recognised in the British Rabbit Council Standards. Points:
30.**
TYPE: As set out for normal textured Rex. Points: 20."
When the Rex was first introduced, it was reckoned to have
sounded the death-knell for all the other fur breeds - but it did not
happen. Likewise with the introduction of the Satin - everything
else was going to become redundant, including Rexes; they were
going to have to satinise to survive. As we all know, whilst the Ivory
Satin has become firmly established, the coloured ones have never
done so, whilst the Satin Rex has not even gained a toe-hold.

Looking back over the years, I can count the number of good
Satin Rexes I have handled on the fingers of one hand:- one very
good Opal, a passable Castor, and one each of Cinnamon, Orange
and Bronze, very attractive but lacking density. One feature stands
out here – they all relied on yellow pigment, which is very much
enhanced by the Satin gene. They were also all smooth coated; the
rough-coated versions I have seen were not properly curled, nor did
such curling as they did possess extend over all of the body, neither
was any sheen in evidence.

Whilst there is a handful of die-hard enthusiasts, I think it must
be said that they are Satin fanciers first and foremost, and the rex
people have never taken to this variety. Primarily, this must be because
the Rex coat, being short and almost at right angles to the skin, will
not show the sheen as a normal coat would.

Secondly, satinisation alters the structure of the hair shaft, resulting
in a tendency to curl, which accounts for the two standards for coat.
The fur generally feels softer and less dense than a normal Rex, and
very many are neither fully smooth nor properly curled. It would be
very easy to say that the Satin-Rex has had its chance, failed, and
should be forgotten, but that would be to overlook a great deal of
potential. Certainly, all the varieties with yellow pigment in their
make-up could become very attractive rabbits if satinised.

Apart from the varieties mentioned above, we would have to include the Lynx and Tortoiseshell, but I would have to recommend that one should concentrate on the smooth-coated versions - the rough ones would appear, on present evidence, to have little in their favour.

Smooth Coated Satin bred by Schlegel and Davies

It is a moot point whether the potential breeder of Satinrex should embark on what might be a lengthy search for stock in the chosen colour; to obtain such stock as may be available in any colour and cross it to that which is desired; or to go right back to basics and produce Rex from the normal. Satinrex are so few and far between that the first option is not really open, unless one is solely interested in the Castor. Here there are at least two small studs from which foundation stock might be obtained, although I am sure they would be the first to admit that there is a great deal of work still to be done.

The second option is, from all practical points of view, also going to involve the Castor, since this is the only colour likely to be obtainable. Mated to whatever colour it is desired to satinise, eventually the object will be achieved, but a very detailed study of the genes involved will be necessary to determine which of the F2 generation to retain for future breeding.

As an example, Castor Satinrex mated to a standard Castor will produce all standard-looking Castors in the F1 generation, assuming that no recessive colours are carried by either parent (which is a big assumption nowadays!). All the progeny will, however, carry the satin gene, so that one in four of the F2 generation will be Satinrex.

The odds become much longer when we introduce a different colour: to produce the Orange Satinrex by this method requires that we mate Orange Rex to Castor Satinrex. This will produce an F1 generation of what appear to be ordinary Castors, but all carrying both the Satin gene and the 'extension of yellow' gene which will produce the Orange.

If you refer back to the chapter on genetics, you should be able to work out that the F2 generation will comprise: 9 Castorex; 3 Orange Rex; 3 Castor Satinrex and one Orange Satinrex. If you can breed a sufficiently large F2 generation, and if Fortune really smiles upon you, you may find that you have sufficient Orange Satins to set up a strain.

More likely, though, is that you only get the odd one, and it will be necessary to use some of the rest of the F2 generation to increase your stock. The Castors will be of no practical use, but two-thirds of the Castor Satins will carry the orange gene, and two-thirds of the Orange Rex will carry the Satin gene. Only a test mating will show whether any animal carries the genes you need - you cannot tell by looking!

Suppose that you find that you have a pair of Castor Satinrex, both known to carry Orange, and a pair of Orange Rex proved to be Satin carriers. If you have managed to breed any Orange Satinrex at all, then you could mate them to either of the two types in the knowledge that fifty percent of the progeny would be of the required variety. In the - more likely - event that the Orange Satinrex has not yet appeared, you might be tempted to mate your Castor Satinrex to the Oranges, but a little thought will show that you still only have a one in sixteen chance of success.

The way to do it is to mate the Castors together, and the Oranges together. Both methods will produce one Orange Satinrex in every four of the progeny.

The final option was to use the normal Satin. In general, the coloured Satins are well behind the Ivories for coat and sheen, and there are very few I would care to introduce into the Rex.

If you should be tempted, remember that, even if the Satin you use is the same colour as the rex, you still have two genes different, and the Satin Rex is only a one in sixteen chance. To use the Ivory is obviously just as big a temptation, to get the coat and sheen. Again, you will get one in sixteen Satinrex in the F2's, but this time you will not be able to predict the colour; as an albino, the Ivory can carry all the other colours hidden, and could probably be relied upon to produce every colour except the one you want!

ROUGH COATED

Astrex
"Fur to be dense, and tightly curled over the whole surface of the body, free from projecting guard hairs. Ears, feet and tail to be well covered with plain fur.

COLOUR: any recognised Rex colour."

The rest of the standard can be summarised as "as for normal coated Rex".

This variety was on the point of being removed from the standards book some years ago, as it was thought to be extinct; then one or two specimens were produced which were thought to be Astrex, so a 'reprieve' was granted.

The curl in the coat is caused by a separate gene, which has no connection with the source of curl in some Satin-rexes. The late Dr Pickard did a great deal of work on this mutation, and found that the gene was a recessive which could be carried by all types of coat,

Astrex, breeder unknown. (John Sandford photo library)

but would only be evident on the Rex.

Furthermore, it only acted fully in the presence of certain modifying genes, which had a tendency to produce a rather soft and curly coat anyway. It is no coincidence that the only Astrex to have attained anything like the correct coats were Blues and Lilacs, or albinos bred from them.

I can, of course, only comment on the Astrex as it was, from the evidence of photographs. The coat looked like Astrakhan fur, and would have had a certain novelty value. I don't think it gained any commercial success with the furriers, as by all accounts it was well-nigh impossible to rear in any numbers. If the early Rexes suffered from poor constitutions, then the Astrex did so to an even greater extent. The majority were completely devoid of hair in the nest, sometimes remaining so until they were three or four months old, needing to be kept in heated quarters; they were also prone to go down with all the ailments known to the fancy, plus a few more of their own!

Type on most was very poor, they generally did not attain their full curl until they were completely adult, and then tended to lose it in the moult: all-in-all, it is a wonder that the Astrex survived as long as it did, which was only a matter of a decade or so.

Then, after being 'extinct' for twenty years or more, it reappeared - or did it? In the course of some experimental breeding involving Brown Beverens, one or two Rexes turned up with a definite curl in the coat, at least at certain stages of their development.

Breeding from these specimens was, to say the least, inconclusive; some of their progeny carried a curl, some did not. In the absence of any of the original mutations, there was no stock available to test whether this was a genuine case of 'throw-back'; a completely new mutation; or just a chance weakness in the fur with no real genetic cause. In view of the fact that no-one who had any of this stock appears to have had any success in 'fixing' the curl, I think we must now, reluctantly, accept that they were not true Astrex.

Nevertheless, we must also accept that this is a recessive gene which could be carried for many generations, by any breed, and could quite possibly reappear at any time if introduced to the Rex. It could also, of course, reappear by a new mutation - history has a

Oppossum, bred by its creator Thomas Leaver

habit of repeating itself, in genetics as in anything else.

There is no practical way of breeding to recover any Astrex genes which may still exist, or to induce a new mutation. All one can say is – and this applies to any major abnormalities – if something turns up in a litter for which you cannot account, always report it to someone who may have the necessary experience to know whether it is of any real significance. The Astrex may quite possibly be dead, but equally possibly it is merely dormant; please don't be the one who discards it if it does reappear!

The Opossum

"**Weight: Adults 6 to 8 lbs.**

Fur: Dense and soft, carried at right angles to the body, without fall, so that from whichever aspect the pelt may be viewed it has the same appearance. The undercoat to be approximately one inch in length. The whole body to be covered with fine white-tipped curly hairs (the curling to

go down to the black undercolour). Bright with lustrous sheen.

Type: Compact body, small near ears, not thin, and carried erect and well covered. Well rounded quarters, without tendency to squareness. Legs straight, medium bone, eyes and toenails to match body.

Colour: Any colour may be recognised, such colour to go right down to the skin. Head, ears, feet and tail not to be silvered, head to be smooth as with ordinary Rex. Silvering to be composed of white-tipped hairs. White hairs to constitute a fault.

Points: As for normal-coated Rex."

I had the good fortune to see what was probably the last of the original strain of Opossum – it looked and felt like nothing so much as an animated hearth-rug! As a curiosity, it made a good talking point but from an exhibition point of view it was next to useless.

The Opossum was evolved by the late Tommy Leaver in Herne Bay, but from what it evolved he never would say. He was supposed to be going to pass on the secret in his will, but never did so; the suspicion must be that he did not really know how he produced them!

Mr Leaver was one of the pioneers with the Fur breeds in this country, with a particular interest in the Argente. I would suspect that the silvering came from the Champagne. There was also in existence until about 1950 a breed called the Chifox, which carried a coat over two inches long, with pronounced guard hairs. This was obviously of Angora derivation: most of the Normal Fur breeds were crossed with the Angora to improve their coats, leading to the production of 'woollies' in most litters for many years.

Chifox were recognised in any colour, so it would have been not unnatural for anyone with an experimental turn of mind to try to silver them. To then 'rex' the silvered Chifox would shorten the coat and give it a tendency to curl at the tips. Since the Chifox had such pronounced guard hairs, they would have tended to curl like the whiskers on a normal rex, and so, I conjecture, the Opossum was produced. On the other hand, Mr Leaver might have had some 'secret weapon' which is now completely lost to the fancy, but I rather doubt it!

To the best of my knowledge, the only person who has ever attempted to re-create the Opossum is my old friend Jimmy Wood of Leven. Jimmy is the inveterate 'champion of lost causes', numbering amongst his many rare variety interests such curiosities as the blue and brown-eyed Ermines. This no doubt accounts for his

Mini Castor Rex. Breeder Brian Roberts

needing over 300 hutches, sufficient justification, surely, for being the only living fancier named in this text!

Jimmy would, I'm sure agree with me that the Argente de Champagne has got to be used and, in the absence now of any Chifox, the Swiss Fox is the only alternative. Whether it would be a better long term prospect to rex the Argente and then lengthen the coat by means of the Swiss Fox, or to silver the Swiss Fox and then rex it is not a question I would even attempt to answer. What has to be said is that, to fit the standard as at present worded, we would have to silver the body alone, leaving the extremities plain - and that strikes me as well-nigh impossible.

Mini-Rex

"The Mini Rex is intended to be a Rex rabbit in every way possible except for its size. It should be judged to the standard of the Standard Sized Rex in all its various colours. Its size shall be approximately half that of the Standard Rex with an ideal weight of 3 to 4 lbs.

DISQUALIFICATIONS - Any rabbit with Netherland Dwarf features. Any rabbit over 4½ lbs."

Here we have the very latest addition to the Rex family, which its proponents would argue has a greater potential to appeal to the ladies and children. One must admit that an eight pound rex is not the easiest of things to handle, and anything which will bring in new recruits to our part of the hobby is to be welcomed.

On the other hand, there are many who feel that the true Rex coat can never be developed on so small a rabbit. It would certainly appear that the majority of Mini-Rex breeders have come to them via other breeds, and not the standard Rexes. Coats, although a lot better than they were a few years ago, have yet to achieve that real plushness, and possibly never will.

The ancestry of our Mini's is rather varied. They are an established breed in the U.S.A., and some may have been imported. Many were derived from the Netherland Dwarf, whilst others have come via breeding from small Standard Rexes.

It is perhaps a sad commentary on the size of today's Rexes that the last course should have been open, but one or two notable successes have been scored that way. I hope the breeders will just bear in mind that an abnormally small rabbit may well carry hidden genes which would have an adverse effect on its breeding potential.

The Dwarf itself is notorious for having few and small litters, and there could be nothing more frustrating than breeding champions which will not reproduce.

Mini Black Rex, fully grown

Whilst quite a lot of Mini's are still well over the four pound mark as adults, their shape in general does conform pretty well to that of a Standard Rex. In some bucks, the head is very large and rounded, which some might say is a Netherland Dwarf feature. On the other hand, there are many Rex breeders who would welcome heads like that; provided that the body shape is correct, I think that such a rabbit is perfectly acceptable.

Coats, as mentioned, have in many cases come close to what is wanted, although there are still a lot which are of obvious Dwarf ancestry, being long, coarse and lacking in density. There is an obvious debate as to whether the coat on a Mini should be half an inch long, or less. If everything is to be kept in proportion, then I suppose they should be shorter, but this is an argument which will run and run.

Colour, as is to be expected at this stage, shows a great deal of variation. Blacks and Ermines are, in general, the closest to the standard, although strangely enough a lot of the Ermines leave a lot to be desired on coat properties. Apart from a couple of very dark Blues, I cannot remember seeing any of the other Self colours.

In the Non-Selfs, there have been one or two very good attempts at the Seal and Sable, in both Marten and Siamese patterns, whilst one young enthusiast in particular has produced very attractive Tortoiseshells. Of the others, most efforts seem to be concentrated on the Castor and Chin. In both colours, we see good type and ever-improving coats, but almost invariably the tops are too dark, and the slate band too wide.

Whilst it is perhaps a little early to be dogmatic, it is possible that the "Wide-Band" gene does not exist in the Mini, and an eventual outcross to the Standard will be necessary. Whilst most shows – and Specialist Clubs – cater for the Mini, in general they come into the same category as the Satin, Astrex and Opossum. Unless special provisions are made in the schedule, they must be shown as A.O.V., whatever their colour.

If they follow the pattern of the Netherland Dwarf and Dwarf Lop they could soon outnumber all the other Fur breeds put together, but to be honest, I believe they will always be regarded as complementary to the Standard Rex and not a substitute.

Harlequin
"(Japanese), English, Dutch etc. - all marked varieties to resemble as nearly as possible the normal varieties in colouring and marking, plus the Rex coat and type."
This small paragraph has caused a great deal of controversy in recent years, as to what is meant by a 'marked variety' and what is

Harlequin bred by Mrs A Dewar

covered by 'etc.' There ought not to be any real controversy: practically by definition, any non-self rabbit is a 'marked variety', whilst 'etc.' means literally 'and others'. The clause was originally intended as a 'catch-all' to enable any known breed to be 'rexed' and shown pending the possible acceptance of an individual standard. With the acceptance of so many new colours and patterns, both in the Rex and in other breeds, the distinction between a 'variety' and a 'colour pattern' is becoming more and more blurred, and it is probably high time that the U.K. Rex Club looked at this paragraph again, to see if it can be better clarified.

The situation as I understand it now is really as it always has been: if a Fancy or Normal Fur breed exists, and has a standard in the book, then the Rex version is allowable, provided that it conforms to Rex coat and type. Thus, the Squirrel and Isabella Rex would be perfectly allowable. A Seal-Point, however, would not be, as it only exists as a pattern within a breed, and not as a variety in itself. If we were breeders of Polish, Netherland Dwarfs or Satins, we could show anything we produced, as long as a standard existed for it somewhere. To this extent we, the pioneers in colour-breeding, have allowed ourselves to be overtaken by others. The advent of the Mini-Rex is bound to introduce new colours - the Seal-Point has already been seen - which by a strict interpretation of the rules would have to go through the whole complicated procedure (and long wait) of official standardisation before they could be shown. When it is only a matter of copying an existing standard, this seems to me totally unnecessary and can hardly be described as 'promoting the exhibition of Rex Rabbits'.

With that bee out of my bonnet, let's consider those varieties specifically mentioned; those which under the current regime should be accepted; those which, like the Seal-Point, cannot be accepted under the present rules; and one or two more which could be produced which have never had a standard, at least in this country.

Harlequin. This is, in fact, one of the oldest Rex patterns, although to the best of my knowledge has never been specialised in. Until comparatively recently the only Harlequins shown came from Normal parentage, and showed it in their coats! Since the advent of the Tricolour Dalmatian, which produces the harlequin pattern as a recessive, the potential to improve the coat quality is there. It is perhaps a sad commentary that the markings of these chance-bred animals are at least as good as if not better than, a lot of the Normals.

English. Another memory of my youth: there was a stud in Northampton which, in a matter of five years or so, managed to get markings on English Rex which were as near to the standard as many Normals. The shorter Rex coats really made the spots stand out, but of course density left a lot to be desired. The owner of this stud, whose name I had better not mention, was never forgiven for giving up the project and taking up racing pigeons; rather than pass on his stock, he killed them all. His name would probably be engraved on a handsome trophy now, had he allowed someone else to carry on his line, but by the time anyone realised what was happening, it was too late. Whilst I have seen a couple since those days, they were really only a Dalmatian with a saddle, and I suppose that if anyone wants a Rex rabbit with spots on, that would be the breed to go for.

Dutch. As with the English, the Rex coat tends to make the markings much more clear-cut, and in the early days of the Rex quite a lot of Dutch appear to have been bred, with some success. As would be expected, the coats took longer to establish than did reasonable markings, but the breed actually died out because of the type! The Rex man naturally pointed to the standard which calls for a 6 - 8 lb rabbit, whilst the Dutchmen wanted one much smaller and cobbier. They felt that only this type could show off the markings properly, and in fact they were right; the Rex type just did not suit the Dutch pattern, the U.K.D.R.C. would not accept the Rex coat and so the breed disappeared. Now, a Dutch-patterned Mini-Rex would be perfectly acceptable - any takers?

Flemish. A ridiculous suggestion you might well say. Put Rex type and coat onto the Flemish Giant and all you have is a steel-grey Rex. The point is that, to the best of my knowledge, this colour has never existed in Rex, but might be attractive to some, and might produce some interesting dilutes! Nevertheless, it would probably be put into the same category as the Seal-Point, and not accepted under the present standard.

Lops. Only mentioned in passing, as I did once see a French Lop with a Rex coat - quite a nice Castor-looking colour. Not acceptable, either as a Lop or a Rex, I'm sure it found a good home somewhere as a pet.

Rhinelander. Somewhat similar to a tricolour Dalmatian, although here a saddle, with both colours showing, is a must. I have never been able to understand why this breed has never at least equalled the English in popularity, and, with its completely different type of coat, it would be much easier to rex. However, I suppose if I were really interested in doing so, I would prefer to start with the Dalmatian and breed a saddle into it.

Silvers. The grey is, of course, the origin of the Silver Seal, and the other colours could be rexed with the same degree of success - i.e., hardly any. Without the guard hairs, it is not a Silver; with them, it is not a Rex.

Thrianta. A tan rabbit but brilliant orange all over, according to the standard. This would equate to the Orange Buff, which has disappeared not only from the show-bench but from the standards book as well. Were there enough Thriantas around, they might be used to re-create the Orange Buff, and even the Tan-Rex. Sadly, they have never become popular; those which are seen tend not to be a good colour, their coats are too long and they are scarcely big enough. Not a good prospect!

Rexed Fur Breeds

Most of the Fur breeds have, of course, already been rexed; those which have not been have been left untouched either for a very good reason, or because they have not been recognised for long enough to gain our attention. In most cases, it would be possible to produce the Rex version from colours which already exist within the Rex, so that in fact it would not be necessary to use the Normal variety at all!

Argentes

We have already discussed these breeds in conjunction with the Silver Seal and the Opossum. There would be no real difficulty in getting the Rex coat onto them, but their attraction comes from the mixture of silver and self-coloured guard hairs, which could hardly be expected to show up on a good Rex coat. I am open to be proved wrong!

Californian

Has quite possibly already been rexed in the guise of the Himalayan, to which standard, of course, it must conform. I only mention the breed since the Lilac-Pointed Himalayan is not yet standardised, so any which were to turn up could only be shown as Californian Rexes!

Beige

"Dark Chamois or light sandy colour, down to the skin, faintly ticked with blue. Hairs tinted light at the base, medium in middle and darker at tips. Blue shading on flanks, muzzle, edges of ears. Top side of hind legs beige, pads blue. Forefeet same as body. Tail being on top, blue under. Belly beige with deeper blue shading."

This is the currently accepted name for the Isabella, which was imported from the Continent in the 1970's, but which never really caught on. I find this rather surprising, as it is a very attractive colour - particularly with a Rex coat on it! The colour is, in fact, the dilute version of the Tortoiseshell, from which several specimens have already been produced. Whilst the extremities are quite definitely blue, the shadings on the body, being caused by guard hairs, are nowhere near as pronounced as on the Normal version. The blue does show up, however as a quite distinct sheen, very attractive to some eyes. The variety must not be confused with a bad-coloured Fawn, which will always have a white belly. This is a pastel-tinted rabbit which could well find favour with the ladies: as such it deserves, and probably needs, its own separate standard.

Perlfee

This is nothing more nor less than the normal-coated version of the Opal, but without the brightness of tanning and definition required in that variety. It might have made more headway had the standard been set to approximate to that of the Opal, but it seems that the continental standard-makers tend to lack the vision of those in this country! I hope that no-one will ever try to produce the Opal by means of the Perlfee.

Squirrel

"Undercolour to be dark slate-blue at base, intermediate portion pearl (slate to be definitely wider than pearl) with blue narrow line edging, pearling to be clearly defined, top grey brightly ticked with blue hairs, either even or wavy ticking admissible; neck fur lighter in colour than the body but strictly confined to nape; flanks and chest ticked with uniform shade of pearl, slightly lighter than body, eye circles light pearl-grey, well defined, ears laced with blue."

This is the blue-dilute version of the Chinchilla, on which the standard has obviously been based, even to the extent of omitting to mention the white belly colour! As a Normal Fur breed, it was never popular and disappeared from the standards book for many years. One or two attempts have been made to produce the Rex version, and I would hope that others might be tempted to try, as it could be even more attractive to some eyes than the Chinrex.

The Squirrel could be re-created, using the Chin-rex as a basis, with the Opal as its opposite partner. Failing this, the Blue, Fawn, Blue Otter or even the Smoke Pearl would have to suffice, although the latter would introduce 'ghosts' and albinos. The odd one or two which have been produced in the past suffered from lack of definition, which is why the use of the Opal is recommended.

Other 'Squirrels'

The dilute, or blue version, is the only one ever to have had a standard of any description, and even that is hardly a satisfactory one for the Rex. It is not, however, the only variation possible on the Chinrex, they could be produced with brown or lilac ticking as well. Apparently the brown version is accepted on the Continent, and there was one which created a great deal of attention in what is now Milton Keynes, forty-odd years ago. Blessed with good type and a really dense coat, this rabbit had an undercolour of brownish slate, a clear pearl band and very light brown ticking on top: it looked like an Ermine which had been lightly dusted with cocoa, and still ranks as one of the most attractive Rexes I ever saw. The owner had a great deal of fun with this rabbit at the smaller shows - it was either best Rex or disqualified every time he showed it! Strictly speaking, it should have been rejected every time, as there was never a standard, but it would be very interesting, to say the least, if one were to appear today. Again the Chinrex would provide a starting point, with either the Cinnamon or Havana to supply the brown genes.

The Lilac Squirrel would be a technical possibility, but would no doubt look too much like a dirty Ermine to make exhibition standard.

Sussex

A recent addition to the Normal Fur breeds, the Gold is, purely as far as colour is concerned, a brown Tortoiseshell, whilst the Cream is the lilac version. Whilst, as yet, no Lilac Points have appeared, the Brown does exist in very small numbers. At present, shadings are conspicuous by their absence, but the body colour is a very pleasing shade of orange, with light brown extremities. Both varieties could legitimately be shown as rexed Sussex but, like their close relative, the Isabella, really need a standard of their own which takes into account the absence of guard hairs.

Seal Points

As a colour-pattern, this first appeared, I believe, in the Netherland Dwarf, and has since become recognised in other breeds - but not, as yet, in the Rex, where they remain confined to 'Unstandardised' classes (which are too few and far between).

At first sight, a poor coloured Himalayan, they are not, in fact, related; the sepia points on the extremities should be the same, but they should also carry sepia shadings on the belly and flanks, and lighter ticking on the back, to give a smoky effect. They are, genetically, chinchillated Tortoiseshells and, as such, could also be produced with blue, brown or lilac points. As a matter of interest, if a brown-pointed Tortoiseshell were used, with the Chinrex, to produce this variety, there would also appear a proportion of Cinnamons and Brown Squirrels - you could fill the A.O.V. class from one litter!

Following the standardisation of the Sallander in 1994, some of the current Seal Points could conceivably be shown as its rexed counterpart. These would be the ones with very dark, "iron-grey" shadings, indicating ancestry from animals carrying the dark chinchillation genes c^{chd} c^{chd}.

Most of the Seal Points in other breeds have much lighter sepia, points and shadings. These must be the result from the light chinchillation gene c^{chl}. As with the Sable and Seal, a considerable difference in colour is apparent between animals with the constitution "c^{chl} c^{chl}" and those which are c^{chl} c (i.e. carrying an albinism gene). These are very light in shade, and have a ruby eye.

JUDGING THE REX

Inevitably, once you have established yourself as an exhibitor, your thoughts will turn to operating on the other side of the table and becoming a judge.

It has often been said that good judges are born, not made; there is a grain of truth in this, but little more. Certainly, if you are the type who dislikes making a decision, or are afraid of expressing an honest opinion for fear of causing offence, you will not be happy behind the judging table. In general though, the person who can correctly interpret the standards and apply them to his own stock has the first requisite to becoming a judge.

Put into its simplest terms, all the judge has to do is to compare two rabbits and decide which of them scores most points out of the allocation of a hundred. If you can do this in the peace and quiet of your own rabbitry, and be satisfied with your own decision, then there is no reason why you should not be able to do the same in a crowded show hall with other people's rabbits.

There are many pitfalls along the road, which I hope to point out, the first one being of course that, the more you judge, the less you will be able to exhibit, so – do you really want to be a judge?

Until comparatively recently, our top all-rounder judges could almost have been called professionals. They could demand first-class rail travel, hotel accommodation and a fee which, in today's values, would be in excess of fifty pounds a day. In many cases the judges were successful businessmen who could have earned at least that by staying at home, so to that extent their charges could be justified.

The other justification was that a top-rank judge would draw a big entry which would more than pay for the cost of his services. That was in the days when stock could be sent cheaply by rail anywhere in the country; those days have long gone and with them any financial inducement to become a judge. Any reward you gain will be to your ego – your self-esteem – and not to your pocket.

Self-esteem may be an outmoded concept in some quarters, but is surely basic to the exhibition of livestock; if you win at a big show with a rabbit you have bred yourself, you can be rightly proud – it was your skill and stockmanship which did it, no effort required by the rabbit! Likewise with judging; you must believe in your own abilities, and regard it as something to be proud of if you are continually asked to demonstrate them.

Accepting that you are not going to be paid as such, don't go to the other extreme and go home out of pocket. By agreeing to judge you have foregone any opportunity of winning prize money, you are at least entitled to claim your necessary expenses, and if you are wise you will agree an approximate figure with the show secretary when you accept the booking.

Whilst most judges make exceptions for their local club or a Specialist Club, the general rule must be to charge reasonable expenses from the very first show. If you are extremely keen to start judging, it may be tempting to offer your services for nothing: don't do it, as that is precisely the value which will be placed on your decisions.

To judge on a regular basis is, in many ways, one of the most satisfying aspects of the rabbit fancy. You will travel to parts of the country you hardly realised existed, handle the best of stock and make far more friends (or enemies!) than you ever would as an exhibitor.

You must be prepared to curtail your own exhibiting but what you must not do is allow judging to become a financial burden.

Probably the biggest difficulty for the novice is to judge according to the standard and not one's own prejudices. Whatever breed we keep, there will always be one or more slight faults which crop up in our own strain which can only be cured by ruthless elimination – they have to be treated as an absolute disqualification as far as our own breeding stock is concerned. Nevertheless, on the show bench, such a fault can only be penalised to the extent which the standard allows.

Whilst it is often said that you can only properly judge a variety if you have bred it, I feel that in many cases the opposite applies. At least, what you will be judging it against. Too often, the so-called "specialist" judge is too influenced by problems he has in his own stock: he will tend to over-promote stock which excels where his own fails and unduly penalise that which carries the same faults as

A well known allrounder judges at a tented show

his own. Both attitudes are wrong, the only standard which should be applied is the one in the book.

In the Rex fancy, one is unlikely ever to become a real "specialist" judge; if you only breed the one variety you will, at best, get the opportunity to judge just that one about once every five years – and then only if you're very good at it. With that little practice, the chances are that you won't be very good at it, so you must get to grips with all the others. This should not be difficult, with very minor exceptions the standard is the same for all of them, colour being the only distinguishing factor.

A much bigger difficulty will be that, at the average show, you will be expected to judge the Normal Fur classes as well, and you must certainly make the effort to understand these breeds. This can only be done by talking about them with as many acknowledged experts as you can, and by handling all types of stock, good, bad and indifferent. You will either soon learn the difference, or find your judging diary strangely empty.

Likewise with the Fancy breeds. Whilst it is highly unlikely that you will be asked to judge them in straight classes, you will certainly have to do so in the duplicates. This is certainly the most difficult aspect of judging; many of the Fancy standards are open to a wide variety of interpretations, and in many cases the judging for Best in Show is like comparing chalk with cheese. However, at most shows it must be done, and you must really study the standards book and be prepared to assess the "opposition" on its merits.

There is a very prevalent attitude, amongst young and old judges alike, that if one is engaged to judge a particular section, one has failed an obligation to the exhibitors unless one's best exhibit is awarded Best in Show.

Nothing could be further from the truth; the judges are there to decide which rabbit most closely approaches its standard. If your nomination is even marginally inferior, you must give way with good grace. In your early days you may fail to spot slight faults in the other rabbits, and have the shortcomings of your own forcibly pointed out; only experience will rectify this. There will be the odd occasion when it is quite literally impossible for you and your co-judge to agree that one rabbit is better than the other – to both minds, both rabbits score identical points. More often you will find that your opposite number can do no more than point out the small patch of moult near the tail which every Fur rabbit will show, whilst expecting you to overlook the fault on his rabbit which will never clear.

In both such cases, the only solution is to ask the Show Manager to appoint a referee. In many cases, the referee will be less experienced than either judge, but that cannot be helped, at least he will – or should be – unbiased.

There are still, unfortunately, a few so-called all-rounders who will never give way, on principle, whatever section they happen to be judging on that day. You will soon get to know these people, and be prepared to call in a referee almost as soon as the rabbits come onto the table! Just accept the situation, don't give way if you're sure you're right, and resolve never to get into that bad habit yourself!

To return to basic principles, sooner or later you are going to be faced with a large straight class – possibly twenty or thirty rabbits – of which seven at the most will get a card.

Whatever you do, don't panic! However long it takes, you have to get them into the right order – even the commended card will have a value to the owner – and you can only do it by methodically comparing one exhibit with another, as if they were the only two rabbits in the class. Some can obviously be sent back to the pen almost as soon as they reach the table, but in most cases a very careful comparison is going to be needed.

The cardinal rule is not to have too many rabbits on the table; if you've only seven cards to award, then there is no point in having more than eight rabbits out at a time. The stewards won't be able to manage them, and you will very quickly lose track of where you have got to. Take your time over the first eight, and the rest will be quite easy.

A professional attitude, integrity and honesty are the hallmarks of the successful judge, and nowhere are these qualities more necessary than in dealing with the 'jockey'.

I am not talking about the obvious novice or over-enthusiastic junior who proudly announce their ownership to all and sundry; a technical infraction of the rules which can easily be righted with a quiet word. There are others a little further up the scale who do no stewarding until their particular class is called: then they suddenly appear at the table and insist on holding one particular rabbit, even to the extent of following it up and down the table as the judge makes his placings.

Yet another type will steward all day, but on occasions will ostentatiously place a rabbit at the head of the table and start to groom it. By his every action he is telling the world that this is his rabbit and he expects it to win, but unless he converts his actions into actual words he cannot be penalised.

In a large class, this type of behaviour can be overcome if the judge works from the other end of the table, or otherwise varies his method of working. It is a very salutary sight to see the expression on the "jockey's" face when he has succeeded in keeping his rabbit at what he thinks is the top of the table only to hear the judge start at the other end with "commended", "highly commended", and "that one down there is V.H.C.!"

The judge must at all times be true to his own conscience; there will be many times when he can be reasonably sure of the ownership of every rabbit on the table. To let that influence the decision in any way is to court disaster; you are there to judge the rabbits, not the owners. Whilst, to the onlooker, it may appear that the "jockey" always wins, it is almost invariably the case that the rabbit would have won anyway, whoever had stewarded it.

In this chapter I have been able to do little more than scratch the surface of the subject. I would strongly recommend anyone interested in judging to read *Rabbit Judgeship* by H D H Dowle. If it is possible to learn how to judge from reading about it, then this is the only book which will help you; if every judge were to follow Mr Dowle's precepts, it would be a happier fancy.

GENETICS AGAIN!

BREEDING SYSTEMS

No book on rabbit keeping would be complete without reference to the various systems used by fanciers to (hopefully) ensure that each generation is better than its predecessor. Generally, these are referred to as 'In-breeding' 'Line Breeding' and 'Outcrossing'. Whilst there is no agreed clear distinction between the first two types, outcrossing is almost self-explanatory so we'll deal with that first.

OUTCROSSING

This is defined as the mating of two animals which are completely unrelated. It will be obvious that, since all Rex can trace a line of descent from one pair of animals, we cannot have a complete outcross by that definition; we would modify it to say that an outcross is between two animals with as little common ancestry as is possible. In practical terms, this would include the mating of animals of two different colours, or two of the same colour which are as completely unrelated as we can get.

In the first case, we might hope that certain aspects of the one colour would combine well with the other, or, more likely, we would be looking to produce a third colour from the first two. In the second case, we would be hoping to bring in certain characteristics from another strain which are absent from our own. There are also those who always claim to use this method, as the mating of close relatives is contrary to the laws of Nature.

This is not true. There are many aspects of animal behaviour which limit the mating of related individuals, but there are probably more which encourage it. Space precludes a more detailed discussion, but we only need to consider the typical herd of deer, pride of lions or even a warren of wild rabbits.

It will be found that each family is headed by a 'dominant' male which, by relentlessly driving off any competitors, ensures that only he gets to mate with the females of the herd. Thus, he will mate with his sisters, daughters, granddaughters – possibly even his own mother. He will continue to do so until defeated by another male; possibly a complete stranger, but much more likely to be one of his own sons. This is Darwinism in its simplest form – the fittest survives;

not just to live, but to reproduce his genes.

In any form of outcrossing, we are combining two sets of genes which, as far as we can arrange, are dissimilar. There are many instances where this widening of the 'gene pool' is to our advantage – it may be the only way to avoid extinction of one particular strain.

In every instance, though, the influence of most of the 'new' genes will be unpredictable. We could, for example, mate two Black Rex, unrelated; we know that all the progeny will be some shade of black, with a rex coat of sorts, but that is all we do know for certain. How well all the other genes involved will combine cannot possibly be predicted – we might have a litter of champions, or complete rubbish.

Outcrossing, as a form of systematic breeding, is a complete non-starter; it is only to be used when all else has failed! Some form of selection must be employed, to concentrate the genes which we want, and to eliminate – as far as we can – those which we don't want. To do this, we must practise some form of inbreeding.

INBREEDING
This involves the mating of individuals which are related – sometimes very closely. The closest relationship is, of course, between brother and sister, father and daughter, and mother and son, and the most extreme form of inbreeding must be the consistent mating together of brother and sister, generation upon generation.

Since each starts off with a set of genes inherited equally from each parent – and the system permits the existence of genes from no other source – it is obvious that a great deal of genetic purity can be established in a very short time. Starting with a pair of animals which together combine all the visible aspects we want to perpetuate, rigorous selection FOR those aspects, and AGAINST those we consider faults, by breeding only from brothers and sisters we could soon establish a strain which possesses only the favourable genes, and so would breed completely true.

That is the theory: to the sceptics, it has to be said that it has also been proved in practice. There have been many instances where brother/sister matings have been carried out for twenty generations or more. The progeny were healthy, grew well and had large litters, as well as looking virtually identical.

This, it must be said, was chiefly because the factors of health, growth rate and fecundity were those selected for. It must also be said that, for every successful inbred strain, there were probably a dozen more strains from the original pairing which died out. They died out because of the accumulation of lethal genes we have already discussed, and this has to be the biggest objection to such close inbreeding as a practical system. We could justifiably include the production of deformities and other abnormalities in the same category as lethal genes, since in the long term they must result in the destruction of the strain.

Lethals and abnormal genes are not the direct result of inbreeding. They occur as the result of mutations, which are no more and no less likely to occur in an inbred strain than they are in any other population. What does happen, of course, is that, if a mutation takes place, or is present in the parent stock, inbreeding will very quickly bring it to the fore.

We have seen in previous sections that a simple recessive gene will be visually evident in a quarter of the progeny of two animals which carry it, and will be transmitted by two-thirds of the remainder. Lethal recessives follow the same pattern. Inbreeding concentrates the genes: the good, the bad, the visible and the invisible. Selection will eventually eliminate the visibly bad ones, but the invisible ones can generally not be detected until it is too late.

To be at all certain of establishing a viable inbred strain from the mating of one pair of animals, we would need to breed a very large number of progeny in the first generation. We would then have to mate a similarly large number of brother/sister pairs, and breed from an equal number of their progeny. The numbers soon progress almost to infinity. Even to reduce to the lowest number of progeny recommended by the scientists – eight to twelve in each generation – would be completely beyond the scope of the fancier, although there might be some application commercially.

To summarise, close inbreeding cannot be considered a practical, long term proposition. It will very quickly establish the favourable genes in our stock, but it will also insidiously accumulate those which will eventually ruin us. Try a brother/sister mating once, after an outcross; this should be regarded as standard practice. Try it again, if this generation is perfectly satisfactory in all respects. Any more will be to tempt Providence! Better then to breed no closer than first cousins, father/daughter or mother/son. This is probably more correctly termed line breeding.

LINE BREEDING

There are almost as many definitions of line breeding as we've had hot dinners! In essence, all systems of line breeding can be defined as 'keeping it in the family'. All animals used are in some way related, but not so closely as they would be in inbred stock.

The simplest of the systems emulates in many ways what happens in Nature. A buck is selected to head the herd. His daughters are mated back to him, so are his grand-daughters, great grand-daughters and so on. This buck continues to be the only one bred from until one of his sons appears to be superior. If the son's progeny proves to be better than those of his father, then the new buck becomes head of the herd and remains so until he himself is usurped.

This is a system very much in use in the horse and dog worlds, where a male animal can exert an influence over a period of many years: a mating to 'Champion so-and-so' can be almost guaranteed to give success, no matter the quality of the female used. Continually breeding back to the original male will result in his likeness being impressed on all subsequent progeny.

As with all systems, there are disadvantages. Naturally, the foundation buck would have to be as near a perfect specimen as possible, and himself be line-bred. If he is genetically pure for all his good points, and these are controlled by dominant genes, he can be expected to pass on all these good points to progeny from even mediocre does. Provided that all his daughters, grand-daughters etc., are returned to him for mating, the line will eventually consist only of animals which are substantially of the same genetic constitution as the foundation buck. We have what is known as a 'pre-potent male', a very useful animal indeed, but an extremely rare one.

Nothing in this life is perfect, and in practice this must include stud bucks! What invariably happens with such a system is that the buck carries a number of recessive genes which are not apparent in his outward appearance. They may not be apparent in his immediate progeny either – unless he is mated to a doe which carries them.

In the second generation, though, any recessive faults will begin to show up; they may be of a comparatively minor nature and become a characteristic of that particular strain, or they may be less immediately noticeable but, in the long run, may result in the extinction of that line. Lethal genes obviously come into this category, as do those which reduce growth rate or even produce abnormalities. They will become established in the strain just as easily as if true inbreeding had been practised. Likewise with the good points; they will become established, and all the progeny will be as good as the original buck – but no better.

Any practical system must take into account two facts. First, that both buck and doe make an equal genetic contribution, and to concentrate only on the genes from one side of the original pairing is to completely neglect any good points which might have been contributed by the other partner.

Secondly, any form of breeding between related animals will concentrate both 'good' genes and 'bad'. Those which merely reduce the 'quality' of a strain as measured against a standard are, at worst, a nuisance. The real 'baddies' are those which gradually reduce the viability of a line; litters get smaller and smaller, and such young as are produced are a bit less healthy, and do not grow so well as their parents or grand-parents.

A cardinal rule must be to only breed from stock which is completely healthy, has come from a large litter, has grown at a steady rate all its life and attained good size and type.

In practice, all these ideals are so hard to attain that we will indeed be tempted to breed from something which was the only one in its litter or which is a very good specimen except that it barely makes the weight as an adult. This has happened on countless occasions, and accounts for the fact that it is hard to establish a winning strain – and even harder to maintain it.

PRACTICAL LINE BREEDING METHODS

Since it must be agreed that outcrossing cannot be the basis for consistently successful breeding, we must accept that the foundation – and maintenance – of a proper 'strain' will involve breeding from animals which are more or less close relatives.

We must also accept that health, litter sizes, growth rates and ultimate size should be our primary concerns: human nature being what it is, I suppose that we also have to accept that eventually we will diverge from those high ideals and be guilty of destroying our 'strain': never mind, it need not be a complete loss, and it will have been fun while it lasted!

FOUNDATIONS

The novice is usually advised to obtain his foundation stock from a single, reputable breeder, or at least from those who have the same strain. This is sound advice, since the majority of stock produced should be of a reasonable quality; whether it is the best way of founding one's own individual strain is open to question.

Much will depend on the genetical purity of that original foundation stock: if it is very pure, there is little or no room for improvement, whereas if the progeny show sufficient variability for improvement to be possible, there is not so much genetical purity and the word 'strain' is hardly warranted.

Take the development of the second type first. We will assume that if all the good points of the progeny could be combined, we would have something near perfection. In such a case, there is no need to bring in genes from elsewhere, we can set up what is known as a "closed herd". All our attention can be concentrated on combining the genes we know we already have; we need not worry too much whether two animals are very closely related or merely distant cousins, we shall eventually be able to trace back through the pedigrees of our champions in a direct line to that original stock.

The question is, do we begin by breeding only the very best animals together – "like to like" – or do we try to balance faults in the buck with excellence from the doe – "pairing of opposites"?

In general, the first course should produce reasonable results fairly quickly. Good points can be expected to be at least maintained, if not improved. Hopefully, the latter will be true and each succeeding generation will be better than the last.

The limiting factors – aside from degeneration due to lethals, etc., – are that eventually we will have 'fixed' all the genes which gave rise to the improvement; the stock will breed true but will get no better in any respect. Also, however good the stock we chose to breed "like to like", it would not have been perfect. By concentrating on the good points, we would inevitably have 'fixed' some bad ones as well.

The second method – pairing of opposites – seeks to overcome this eventuality. Animals are chosen so that the failings of one are counterbalanced by the good points of the other.

Clearly, if the failings are caused – as they often are – by recessive genes, the next generation must show a distinct improvement. The recessives will still be there, of course, but their effect will be gradually reduced over a period of time. It is this method which most fanciers use; balance is all-important, and provided that all faults on one side are counterbalanced on the other, there should be a gradual improvement in all aspects with succeeding generations. The faults will become less and less serious and should eventually disappear from most of the stock.

That all sounds very easy, it might seem that anyone could have a shed full of potential Bradford winners in only their second or third year of breeding. Sometimes it is easy, as the success of many relative novices has proved. There are, though, limiting factors with this method just as there are with others.

Firstly, we need to set ourselves some very stringent standards. The bad points can certainly be counterbalanced by the good – but the reverse is also true. If one of the pair has a very good colour, it must be accepted that this is caused by an accumulation of favourable modifying genes. When mated to its partner which is not so good a colour, the genes will be diluted, and the colour of the progeny, whilst better than one parent, will not be so good as that of the other. Therefore, if we are to breed at all from an animal which is faulty on one point, it must be well above average in all other respects. Its partner must also be well above average in these respects, and not merely be better on the point we are trying to improve, but must really excel. The progeny can then be expected to be above average in all respects, and have the potential to improve further on the point where one parent excelled.

This, I agree, is somewhat Utopian. Most animals which excel in one point will not be above average on everything else, but will have a slight fault somewhere. In that case we are looking for a partner which excels on that point, but may not be so good on the first, so we have two points to counterbalance. Even if the 'good' points are caused by simple dominant genes, there is no better than a fifty percent chance that we can get them both on the same animal. In practice, modifiers play such a big role that we can only set certain basic ground rules, and let the law of averages take care of the rest. Firstly, we must stress that if there is any doubt about the health, size or fecundity of any animal, it should not be bred from, however good it may appear in other respects.

Secondly, we must set as high a standard as possible for all the physical attributes we are concerned with. Granted that not all of our stock will score the full forty points for colour, we must be prepared to say that anything which scores less than, say, thirty will not be used, however good it is otherwise. As time goes on, we must continually raise our standards, otherwise the only result will be mediocrity. The excellence with which we started will have been far too diluted to be recoverable.

Thirdly, we must be prepared to set up more than one line. On the basis that type only accounts for twenty points, we might set ourselves a relatively minimal standard there, but pay much more attention to coat and colour. A line could be established where the object was excellent colour, but just acceptable coat, and another line which excelled on coat but was not so good on colour. It would be absolutely vital that each line were continued until it were true breeding. The hope would be that, by combining the two lines, our stock would then excel in both coat and colour and we could divert our attention to improving the type.

We would, upon reflection, have wished that we had paid more attention to type in the first place! This is by far the easiest characteristic to fix and we should certainly have done so. It is to be as common an attribute to our two lines as health and fecundity, and no failing should be tolerated.

It will be obvious by now that no one method of breeding can be guaranteed to give lasting success if used to the exclusion of all others. Indeed, it could be said that our aims, as exhibiting fanciers, to some extent preclude our developing any one system to the ultimate.

Very few fanciers would have the patience to embark on a course of breeding in the certain knowledge that they would have nothing good enough to show for at least five years. Most would not plan a mating unless they felt there should be a chance of a show rabbit in the expected litter, and to that extent most of our breeding is a compromise. A rabbit which excels in one point will usually be faulty elsewhere, and invariably be beaten by one which is just good all round, without excelling anywhere.

Yet, in the long run, it is the points of excellence which we must perpetuate: to get them established we must either forgo exhibiting for a while, or set up a system which will, hopefully, give us the best of both worlds.

THE ROAD TO UTOPIA

The fancier who wishes to really make a name for himself must be prepared to question established wisdom at every step, and never more so than at the very beginning of the exercise. By convention, we are told to get all our stock from a successful breeder, of as high a quality as the purse will allow.

There is nothing wrong with this advice, particularly for the novice, but the original breeder will always be one step ahead of you however much money you have paid.

Therefore, it must make sense to get stock from two different sources. Even a mated doe from two different strains should enable us to keep both lines going in our rabbitry, and give us something to show whilst we embark on the real object of the exercise, which is to combine the good points of both strains to establish our own. To do this, we will have to use all three methods of breeding, beginning with the outcross.

FIRST GENERATION

As we have already seen, the initial results of an outcross are entirely unpredictable; the progeny may look excellent, or they may appear to be rubbish. One thing is almost certain, though; they will be healthier and grow quicker than either of the line-bred strains.

"HYBRID VIGOUR"

Any form of systematic breeding tends to concentrate "lethal" genes, as we have seen and, equally, it must also tend to concentrate those which limit growth rates. As fanciers rather than commercial breeders, we do not give these points the attention which we undoubtedly should do, with the result that the adverse recessive genes become established eventually in every strain.

The important point to note is that there are probably hundreds of genes which affect growth rate and fecundity, and the chances are that the genes which cause a deterioration in one strain are entirely different from those which produce the same effects in another.

When the two strains are combined, the two sets of recessives are masked, so we can confidently expect the first litters to contain a lot more young than we are accustomed to, and that the progeny will be much healthier and grow more quickly. The recessive genes will still be carried, it is up to us to ensure that they do not become a danger to future generations.

SECOND GENERATION

Our first generation will, between them, carry all the genes from the two foundation strains. It is no use whatsoever just to take what appear to be the two most promising animals and breed from them, since it is practically impossible that between them they carry every possible combination of genes. The object must be to breed from everything which is not obviously unhealthy or of faulty conformation. We need as large a second generation as possible, with a very large gene pool, and to do this we must breed brother to sister, from as many combinations as we can accommodate.

It is at this stage that most attempts to found a strain begin to go astray; a great many progeny must be raised to maturity, and the average fancier just does not allow enough space.

Only when this generation is fully adult can we begin to make any meaningful selection. We can eliminate any which have not grown well, and we must also eliminate any with poor type. Of the rest, some will be above average for coat, some above average for colour.

The temptation must be, by the mating of opposites, to attempt to produce show specimens in the third generation. This, in my view, would be a big mistake; we should still have the two original strains to give us a few for show, and our object should really be to further improve the good points from our second generation.

It was stressed earlier that the mating of opposites would only be really successful if one partner excelled on a particular point. We can go further and say that the excellence is only of real use if it can be passed on – that is, 'fixed', which means line-breeding, like to like, until we have developed that particular attribute to its utmost. Hence, we have at least two separate lines to set up. In the simplest possible case, one will excel in colour, the other in coat.

There are, of course, many separate aspects to both coat and colour, and it would be a fortunate – and wealthy fancier who could afford to set up several different lines, each breeding true for one particular aspect in which it excels.

In practical terms, though, two lines should suffice. Within the 'colour' line, some may well be better for top-colour than undercolour for example, whilst in the 'coat' line some might excel in density, others in texture. The salient point is that each rabbit used for breeding must EXCEL somewhere, and selective breeding purely for colour in one line, and coat in the other, will tend to fix the excellent points much more quickly and effectively than if the attempt had been made with just one line.

Within each line, should we inbreed or not? Quite frankly, it doesn't really matter: the object must to be 'fix' the desirable points, and this will be much more quickly achieved by mating closely related animals.

On the other hand, those lethal genes are still lurking around, just waiting to be 'fixed' as well.

It would be foolish to refuse to mate two excellent animals just because they were both brother and sister, but even more foolish to breed from their progeny if there was the slightest doubt regarding litter sizes and growth rates. The best advice is that if two rabbits look as if they should produce the goods, give them a chance, regardless of relationship – but don't give them a second chance if there is the smallest sign of 'lethals' becoming established.

It may well take five years or more before we can safely say that our two lines are true breeding: what next? We could, of course, now begin to select the best coated specimens from the 'colour' line, knowing that good colour had been fixed, and likewise for colour from the 'coat' line In practice, though, the necessary genes in each line may well not be there, and we must combine the two.

We are now in an exactly similar situation to that described in the chapter on the Tan. The hope is that the union of the two lines will produce animals which excel both in coat and colour and, indeed, there is every chance that they will. For a time, at least, your strain should be unbeatable (unless, like me, you always sell the wrong rabbits!) but the battle is by no means over.

The excellent all-round specimens you have produced will not breed true, since they carry 'poor' and well as 'excellent' genes for both coat and colour. There will not, however, be such a wide variation as there was when the original two strains were crossed, and a fair proportion of their progeny would be good show specimens.

Nevertheless, they are unlikely to really excel on all points, so the object must be to retain – and further develop – the two lines you have spent all those years establishing. The progeny may well be extremely valuable show stock – but the parents are priceless!

MUTATIONS

In an effort to make this section understandable to everyone, I have kept the technicalities to a minimum. We have concentrated on what a gene does, rather than what it is, hence we cannot really define a mutation other than by the effect it shows; still less can we say that causes it.

What we can say, being truthful and at the same time not too technical, is that a gene is a code – a computer programme if you wish. It controls one particular function in every individual cell in the body of the animal and has the unique ability to replicate itself whenever the cell divides – hence its continuing effect, via the gene cells, on future generations. As long as each replicated gene is a "carbon copy" of its originator, the characteristic which it controls will be transmitted unchanged.

However, even in the best regulated circles, accidents can happen. Very rarely – but often enough to be significant – a gene does not produce a perfect copy of itself with the result that it passes on a changed characteristic. We have seen, in the rex coat, an example of how such a change can be 'fixed' in a population.

What we cannot tell with any certainty is what causes a particular gene to change, or "mutate". Some forms of disease have been proved to give rise to an increased rate of mutation, as have most types of radiation: hence the reluctance of doctors to use X-Rays on pregnant women.

What caused the rex mutations is very much a matter of speculation, although many of the first researchers felt that the bacillus "spirochaetes" was a prime suspect, as it was proved to be present in much of the stock in that area of France.

There can never be any positive proof, one way or the other, but it does give rise to one beautiful thought. This is the bacillus which causes syphilis in humans, and as such has been responsible for much misery. Could it, at the same time, have been responsible for two of the greatest pleasures known to Man – the Rex coat and the music of Schubert?

APPENDIX

FAMILY TREE

"X" signifies a combination lacking exhibition potential.

	$C+E+$	$c^{chd+}E^+$	$c^{chl+}E^+$	C^+ee	$c^{chd+}ee$	$c^{chl+}ee$	
$A+$	Castor	Chin	X	Orange (1)	X	X	$B+D+$
$A+$	Cinnamon	(Brown Squirrel)	X	Orange (2)	X	X	$bbD+$
$A+$	Opal	Squirrel	X	Fawn (1)	X	X	$B+dd$
$A+$	Lynx	(Lilac Squirrel)	X	Fawn (2)	X	X	$bbdd$
a^{t+}	Black Otter/Tan	Black Fox	Marten Seal *	Orange Buff(1)	X	X	$B+D+$
a^{t+}	Chocolate Otter/Tan	Chocolate Fox	X	Orange Buff(2)	X	X	$bbD+$
a^{t+}	Blue Otter/Tan	Blue Fox	Marten Smoke *	X	X	X	$B+dd$
a^{t+}	Lilac Otter/Tan	Lilac Fox	X	X	X	X	$bbdd$
aa	Black	X	Seal *	Tortoiseshell	Iron Grey	Seal Point	$B+D+$
aa	Havana	X	(Possibly Nutria)	Sussex Brown	Brown Sealpoint	Brown Sealpoint	$bbD+$
aa	Blue	X	Smoke Pearl *	Beige	Blue Sealpoint	Blue Sealpoint	$B+dd$
aa	Lilac	X	X	Sussex Cream	Lilac Sealpoint	Lilac Sealpoint	$bbdd$

This is a much simplified diagram showing the major genetic relationships within the Rex breeds.

As an example, we can see that the Lilac has the primary genes aa bb CC dd EE, and that the rabbit with genetic constitution A+ B+dd E+ is an Opal.

Refer to the text for the inheritance of the Dalmatian, Harlequin and Himalayan patterns.

*   With the addition of the simple albinism gene (c), this becomes the light or medium shade of Sable or Smoke Pearl. See the text for further explanation.

Further Reading

The following titles may be of interest to the rex fancier; regrettably several – including the classic *The Domestic Rabbit* – are out of print. Source second-hand bookshops or the internet, or contact Veronica Mayhew, Trewena, Behoes Lane, Woodcote, Nr Reading, RG8 OPP (01491 680743) email: *veronica.mayhew@virgin.net* who specialises in old and out of print rabbit books and prints.

Fur & Feather stocks around thirty recommended rabbit titles in their postal bookshop; for a copy of their book list telephone 01473 652 789 or contact the address below.

REX BREEDS
The Rex Breeds of Rabbit edited by Capt W Brumwell, Watmoughs Ltd., 1931
Dalmatian Rex Rabbits by Roger Hutchings, Maverick Editions, 1993
Read About Rabbits: Rex by Alwyn Scott and Harry Bush, Winckley Publishing, 1983

GENERAL
The Domestic Rabbit by J C Sandford, Blackwell Science, 5th Edition 1996
British Rabbit Council Breed Standards, paperback free to members, or with colour photographs in binder, price on application. (Purefoy House, 7 Kirkgate, Newark, Notts NG24 1AD)
Exhibition & Pet Rabbits by Meg Brown, Spur Publications,1978
Rabbit Lopaedia by Meg Brown and Virginia Richardson, Interpet, 2000.
Encyclopaedia of Rabbits & Rodents by Esther Verhoef-Verhallen, Rebo Productions, 1977.
Rabbit Breeding for Perfection by A E Williams, Acacia Press, 1992
Rabbit Judgeship by H D H Dowle, Coney Press, 1992
Rabbits, Health, Husbandry and Diseases by Virginia Richardson, Blackwells, 2000
Diseases of Domestic Rabbits by Lieve Okerman, Blackwell Science, 1994
Textbook of Rabbit Medicine by Frances Harcourt-Brown, Butterworth Heinmann, 2002
Greenfoods for Rabbits and Cavies by F R Bell, Watmoughs, 1978
Rabbit Nutrition by Virginia Richardson, Coney Press
Colour Inheritance in Small Livestock by Roy Robinson, Watmoughs, 1978
Practical Inbreeding by W Watmough, Winckley Publications, 1990
Rabbit Production by Cheeke, Lukefahr, Patton, McNitt, The Interstate Publishers & Printers, 1987
The Biology of the Laboratory Rabbit by Weisbroth, Flatt and Kraus, Academic Press, New York, 1974
Laboratory Animal Medicine edited by Fox, Cohen, Loew, Academic Press, New York, 1984

Photographs:
All photographs from *Fur & Feather* archives and the John Sandford photo collection, except for page 68 (by permission of Alwyn Scott); Opal rex on page 10 (by permission of Harry Hopkinson); pages 23 and 24 (rabbit shed and block of hutches) by permission of Dennis Arrand.

UK Rabbit Governing Body, Magazine, Clubs

British Rabbit Council, Purefoy House, 7 Kirkgate, Newark, Notts. NG24 1AD. Phone 01636 676042. Fax 01636 611683. Email: info@thebrc.org. Web Site: www.thebrc.org.

The BRC is the governing body of the rabbit fancy, issuing show support to affiliated clubs and rings to its members. It publishes a Breed Standards book – see page 59.

Fur & Feather inc. RABBITS, Elder House, Chattisham, Ipswich, Suffolk IP8 3QE. Phone 01473 652 789 or 01473 652 354. Fax 01473 652 788. Email: furandfeather@btinternet.com.

Web Sites: www.furandfeather.co.uk and www.rabbitsmagazine co.uk.

Fur & Feather inc RABBITS is the official journal of the British Rabbit Council.

Clubs: The following were affiliated to the British Rabbit Council at time of publication. Contact addresses can be obtained from the British Rabbit Council, Purefoy House, 7 Kirkgate, Newark, Notts. NG24 1AD.

National Rex Clubs:

United Kingdom Rex Club. Caters for all colours of rex.
National Black Rex Club.
National Blue Rex Club.
National Castor Rex Club.
National Chinrex Club.
National Dalmatian Rex Rabbit Club.
National Ermine Rex Rabbit Club.
National Havana Club.
National Himalayan Rex Rabbit Club.
National Lilac Club.
National Lynx Rex Club.
National Mini Rex Rabbit Club.
National Orange & Fawn Rex Rabbit Association.
National Otter Rex Rabbit Club.
National Seal & Sable Rex Rabbit Club.

AREA REX CLUBS

Beds, Herts & Bucks Rex Rabbit Club.
Eastern Counties Rex Rabbit Club.
Essex Rex Club.
Kent Rex Rabbit Club.
Midland Rex Club.
North Eastern Rex Rabbit Club.
Northern Rex Rabbit Association.
Scottish Rex Rabbit Club.
Southern & South Western Rex Rabbit Club.